Stories of Coming Home

Finding Spirituality in Our Messy Lives

William John Fitzgerald

PAULIST PRESS
New York ✦ Mahwah, N.J.

Cover design by Duffi Goodrich
Book design by Cynthia Dunne

LIBRARY OF CONGRESS CATALOGING-IN-PUBLICATION DATA

Fitzgerald, William, 1932–

Stories of coming home : finding spirituality in our messy lives / William John Fitzgerald.

p.   cm.

Includes bibliographical references.

ISBN 0-8091-3752-6 (alk. paper)

1. Spiritual life —Catholic Church. 2. Reconciliation—Religious aspects —Catholic Church. I Title.

BX2350.2.F499   1997

248.4'82 —dc21   97-40026

CIP

Published by Paulist Press

997 Macarthur Boulevard

Mahwah, New Jersey 07430

Printed and bound in the

United States of America

Contents

Dedicated to:
Barbara Heaney, M.D.
John Hartigan, M.D.
Larry Gillick, S.J.
Healers of bodies/spirits

and to
Jane, Dick, Louise,
Rich, and all my other
"Spirit Companions"

With deep appreciation
to my editor,
Maria Maggi who made
sense out of my
messiness,
and Jeannie Beal who
helped proof the crooked
lines straight.

Prayers and Reflections

Introduction

Invariably, when friends have asked me about the title of this book, they smile when I tell them it is a book for messy or messed up Catholics and their friends. "Really?" they say. And when I tell them it is all about spirituality in the midst of messiness, they give a similar response. They smile again, and say, "Messiness! I think I could use that kind of book!"

If you or your loved ones have experienced messiness, or chaos, this book is for you. If you or any of your loved ones or friends are messy or messed up Catholics, this book is about helping you or them come home to find pastoral care and deeper spirituality.

It is really an old story. The Spirit (Breath) of God entering into our messy and sometimes chaotic life stories goes back to the very beginning as we read in the book of Genesis:

…God created the heavens and the earth, the earth was a formless void and darkness covered the face of the deep while a wind from God swept over the face of the waters. (Gn 1:1–2) [1]

From the very beginning, it seems that the wind—the breath of God who is the Spirit—has enjoyed messing around with chaos and calling forth something new out of disorder. This is true for the cosmic story and it can be true for our human stories as well.

This book is about coming home from a Spirit-filled journey through confusion and darkness. The chapters ahead come out of a pastor's journal, kept as it were in the trenches of parish life. It is about pastoral care for messy and chaotic lives—finding the spark of the Spirit in the dark.

Arnold Mindell writes:
An entire book should be devoted to the public's need for the dark side of life…this is where the gold lies. [2]

This book is about bringing home from darkness, messiness, and chaos the golden, bright treasure of the Spirit. In this book *spirituality* means the invaluable treasure that lies at our deepest core—that divine spark which illumines the beauty of creation and provides our spiritual energy, our deeper meaning, and our transcendent destiny.

THE SPIRIT IN THE MIDST OF GRIT

Like gold in a stream, our spirituality may be surrounded by grit, or like gold in a mine, enveloped in darkness. However, spirituality in messiness means that we can pass through the dark, mine treasure from it, and come home again enriched in the Spirit.

At first glance, "messiness" and "spirituality" seem like contradictory terms. Quite to the contrary, it is the premise of this book that the Spirit of God can be present deep down and all around in the brokenness and chaos of our human lives. This same Spirit calls us home to find a deeper spirituality as we encounter turmoil in the stories of ourselves, our families, our mother the earth and our mother church.

JESUS AND MESSINESS

The Jesus you will encounter in the following reflections is the sweaty Jesus who made friends with chaos and disorder and brought forth a new creation from the pregnant darkness of the tomb.

This is the Jesus we discover on the muddy river bank, honoring the unkempt John the Baptist. It is the Jesus who encountered and loved the fishy fishermen, the stinking Lazarus, the repulsive lepers, and the young couple who ran out of wine at a poorly organized wedding feast. It is the Jesus who knew something good could come from mud, and who smeared it on the blind man's eyes. This is the Jesus who came to save the many who did not seem to have their act together. The example of Jesus suggests that we can find treasure even in the murkiness and chaos of our lives.

COMING HOME

The Catholic story is a coming home story. Our church is mother church. Her clergy are father, sister, brother. Her greatest glory is her family meal. Attend a gathering of older Catholics talking about the old days, and the question often arises, "What was your *home* parish?"

Our church is not a perfect housekeeper. We all leave muddy tracks on her carpets! However, the Catholic story always accepts muddy earthiness because Jesus took the earth seriously and was nourished and formed from it. Our Catholic imagery is at its best when, on Ash Wednesday, we are smudged with earth; at Easter, doused with water; and at Christmas, led to a messy crib. At our funeral liturgy, when our life story is complete, we shall be incensed with fragrant smoke and assured that we are to be led home by the messy, sore-infested beggar, Lazarus.

May the angels lead you into paradise, the martyrs come to meet you, and with Lazarus, who was poor, may you have eternal rest. [3]

These are all reasons why this book is titled, *Stories of Coming Home—Finding Spirituality in Our Messy Lives.*

IMAGES, STORIES, AND PRAYERS

"A picture is worth a thousand words." So the old saying goes. As I do in my preaching, in the following chapters I sometimes use images from films to illustrate our search for meaning in our messy stories. I do so because I notice people perk up and listen when I make movie connections in homilies. As I also do in preaching, I use illustrations from my pastoral experience.

The text of each chapter is meant to be interactive. There are reflection pauses within the text. They are there to enable you to pause, pray, and relate the text to your own sometimes messy life situation. There are also prayers, scripture references, and reflection questions that might be used as journal-starters. These are found at the end of each chapter.

If you know people who feel lost, outside, or messed up, you might share this book with them, for in our Father's house, there are many rooms, and all of us can come home again.

1

Coming Home to Spirituality Through Our Messy Stories

If spirituality means connecting with the divine energy and its meaning for our lives, then where are we to find the Spirit? Amazingly, the Spirit seems to dwell in the midst of our messy human stories. The Spirit makes His or Her home deep down in human experience—which is often confusing and sometimes alienating. Yet in the dark chapters of our life stories, the Spirit can console us and we can be drawn away from alienation toward union and communion. The creative impulse of the Spirit may even initiate a change in our life scripts. We can come home to the Spirit through the messy stories of our lives.

So many of us leave home on our heroic quests for a life work or an adventure, for new relationships and greater challenges. Sooner or later—in the unfolding of our life stories, in the midst of our coming and going—our spirit often thirsts for something more. Viktor Frankl, who spent torturous months in a World War II concentration camp, wrote that the deepest need in our human story is not power, nor sex; it is our need for meaning.

If we are to come home to find our spirituality—our deepest meaning—we must pass through messiness to get there. A muddled sense of alienation is part of our human condition. We discover it within ourselves, among ourselves, and in the images of drama, television news, and sports that portray our stories. This very messiness, however, can provide a flash point for something new and creative. Spirit companions can help us find the way through the worst of chaos and help us to live with the rest of the mess. Our journey through turmoil is sometimes a heroic struggle, but it can transform us. It can bring us home.

Sometimes, we have to look back in time at our own stories as well as at the lives of the saints to discover what our story means and how the Spirit works in the midst of messiness.

BILLY

The year was 1948. Billy, a frail only child, was a freshman at an all boys Jesuit high school. Too scrawny to make a mark in athletics but wishing to be close to the action, he volunteered to be the bat boy for the American Legion summer team made up of juniors and seniors from the high school. They were the Murphys sponsored by a local car dealer. Billy would never earn an athletic letter at the high school, but he wore quite proudly the blue Murphy baseball cap emblazoned with its white M. A high point of the summer would be the annual road trip out into midwestern towns. There would be heavy bat bags to tote, but that would be a labor of love for this youngster so enamored with every sport.

This road trip would be his first journey not made with family. He would be the freshman runt among this litter of junior and senior ballplayers. The first night started with a glow. The Murphys won their first game, and then checked into the city's Main Street hotel.

After the game, the players milled around the lobby and then started drifting out onto the streets to explore the town. Billy skipped along like an anticipating pup. It was a new adventure. Block by block, the ball players broke up into smaller groups sifting off into side streets. Soon, it was just Billy and two of the ball players. They found themselves at a fence. Just beyond, the moon gleamed off the surface of the town's swimming pool. The gate was securely locked. One ball player said to the other, "I think we can make it over the fence. Let's take a swim." With some difficulty, they climbed over. Billy tried, but he got up only half-way. "Hey, wait for me!"

There was laughter for awhile, then splashing, and after that, silence. Billy waited and waited for them to return, but they never came. They had found another exit on the other side of the pool and had slipped away from him. It was approaching midnight. Billy didn't know where he was, but he did know that they were not coming back. He had been ditched. Whatever lostness feels like, he was beginning to experience it at this swimming pool fence. Not only was the pool empty—so was his inner spirit. His own excitement vanished with his companions. All that remained was a humiliating sense of being left out, a pain that many adolescents have experienced at one time or another. Such an experience is especially sharp and cutting for a young teen who desperately wants to belong to a peer group. So, as he walked along the streets of this strange town he found himself alone in an alien place for the first time in his thirteen years. Small creaking noises came from securely locked houses. They were locked in their homes. He was locked out of life.

Shadows reached out like grasping fingers. He was cast into the outer darkness, but also into his own inner darkness. He was left to shift for himself in a strange place. His inner ache was enormous; it was a combination of turmoil and hurt pride. He was angry and ashamed. He had thought that he was a Murphy, but now the name did not fit. How could they do this? He only wanted to tag along with them. The darkness gave him permission to do that last thing any teenage boy could not bear to do, to weep bitter tears. He was experiencing for the first time the agonizing pain of alienation, an experience deeper than loneliness. It was a lostness, a displacement, a disconnection, a sense of rejection, the chaos blocking the way to coming home.

His journey through the dark had now initiated him to the *via dolorosa*—the path of sorrow. That night, as he stumbled through the dark, he would finally find his way home to the hotel only through a combination of trial and error—up one street and down another, backing up and starting over until, at last, remembered landmarks pointed the way.

It would be many years later that he would begin to realize that his pain had been the tiniest hint of the agony of alienation experienced by so many all around him. He had yet to learn about racism, tribalism, sexism, fundamentalism, the *isms* that divide people. Nor was he aware of the pain people face through abuse, divorce, separation, loss of employment and the many other life experiences that shut out people.

He would discover much later that this painful night was probably the beginning of his adolescent passage, a route of discovery. The name of that city was appropriate. It was Columbus.

He returned to school that fall and his rite of passage continued by way of a breakthrough experience. A teacher cajoled and encouraged him to sing a song at an assembly attended by the 500 boys in the high school. The upper classmen who had ditched him a month before would be there in that all-classes assembly. As he stepped onto the stage, all he could see were glaring lights, but he knew there was a boisterous crew lurking in the shadows. He did not know how they would respond. For him, at that moment, they seemed more like a potential firing squad than an audience. He sang his song. He gave it his best. Then there was a moment of truth. They might have hooted and turned thumbs down like the Roman crowds in the colosseum. They were, after all, an unpredictable cauldron of young male energy. They did not. Instead they gave him a rousing and sustained roar of applause. They demanded an encore!

When he experienced their applause, he was home free! Their response was a critical flash point. In that moment, he sensed a shift within himself. It was a leap from alienation to reconciliation. He was lost, and now he was found. As shy and inhibited as he was, a rejection at that critical moment might well have dissuaded him from ever attempting again to stand before a group. Later in life, he would credit his ability to speak to crowds in cathedrals, on television, and at national workshops to that critical breakthrough moment in his youth.

From that point on, he would blend in with his own classmates. To his surprise, they would elect him to several offices. He never earned an athletic letter; it was not his gift, but he would be a part of the diverse mix of talents and energies that made up his class. He would never be Billy again; they would nickname him Fitz, a badge of acceptance and comradeship.

Forty years later, he would walk into a reunion with his classmates and sense immediately that he had come home again. After the handshakes, the story swapping, and the banqueting, the emcee arose and announced, "We'd like a few words from Fitz, and maybe a song." Forty-four years before, his alienation had been to walk through the dark night, unnamed, unchosen, and ashamed. When that gang of boys applauded, they gave him a gift of "Thanks!" and even more.

David Steindl-Rast, writing about gratitude, says,
One single gift acknowledged in gratefulness has power to dissolve the ties of our alienation, and we are home free—home where all depend on all. [4]

That night on the stage, so long ago, was a breakthrough event that named him as one of them—at home with them—"where all depend on all."

A SHARED STORY

That was my adolescent story, the journey from Billy to Fitz, from being messed up with shame and alienation to the homecoming marked by acceptance and reconciliation. At the flash point between alienation and reconciliation, I had experienced a surge of growth and development. I had been shamed, but had managed to sail free. After years of pastoral work, I believe it is in some variation the story of most of the people I meet. It is the messy alienation/reconciliation story. So many people experience alienation and the shame that sometimes follows. So many are locked out. So many walk alone down a shadowy inner path. Alienation is within and without. So many yearn to find the way home and seem to find the doors shut. Too many have entered the baptismal font, only later to find the gate to life-giving waters has been padlocked. It is too often that dry-dock, rather than sailing free, seems to be our destiny.

REFLECTION PAUSE

Who do you know who stands at the swimming pool gate like Billy did, somewhat lost, and longing to get in? Imagine the Lord there, unlocking the gate and leading them in to refreshing waters. Speak to the Lord about them.

FENCED OUT FROM HAPPINESS

Sometimes we may expect someone else to pull us over the fence and into the calm pool of perfect happiness. We can become even more alienated and disappointed when this friend or this mate cannot deliver on our high expectations.

When we feel belittled, as Billy was at the swimming pool gate, or abandoned by significant others, or, worse yet, traumatized by abuse, we can feel very hollow and empty. We may open the door to addictions which promise FULL-fillment, only to find that they fill the body and empty the soul.

CARE UNITS

Yet, for some in the murky night, intensive CARE UNITS offer shelter. They have their wards where the wounded find companions for their journeys. Alcoholics Anonymous and the other recovery groups provide today's great rites of passage. A.A.'s way out—or way through—is twelve steps in the right direction: one day at a time, with companions who have been down the road. There has never been a religious procession more holy, healing, or reconciling than that of the various recovery groups. They bring journeyers home to themselves and to their God.

ALL IN A MESS, ONE WAY OR ANOTHER

Some of us may not recognize our messiness as clearly as those making the recovery journeys. We may weave between alienation and reconciliation. Sometimes our turmoil gathers force like a cyclone and becomes chaos. When I experienced that messy teenage night, it was but a hint of the chaos that could and would later erupt in my adult life.

TEARS THAT WASH AWAY CHAOS

If my self-pitying and childish tears at the swimming pool gate were a necessary adolescent rite of passage through messiness, then my own tears for my serious personal failings and sins later on in my adult life would be the beginning of a passage through sinful chaos. (Real sin—my own, yours, or other's is one of the major producers of chaos in our life stories.)

When we bring sinful chaos into our own and into other people's lives, only tears can begin to wash away the debris that litters our road home. Tears may mess up our faces, but they cleanse our souls. How wonderful it is that cleansing rain can emerge from lightning and boiling clouds. So can holy tears emerge from the midst of our own chaos. They can call us home to our true and deepest self where the Spirit dwells.

Each of us can come home again to the dynamic Spirit capable of bringing us consolation, a sense of unity and community, and even new creativity in the midst of messiness. As we pass through messiness, the Spirit can change our lives. We can begin the journey home again by reflecting prayerfully on our messy stories.

OUR WILDERNESS

Being locked out, separated, alienated, wounded, needing to find our way home is as old as the lock-out at Eden, and as new as the social walls separating suburbia and the inner city, the establishment and the immigrant, the economic winners and losers, the married and the widowed, the straight and the gay.

We experience alienation and separation in our personal life stories sometimes through our own sinfulness but at other times through the death of loved ones, job losses, corporate dislocations, misunderstandings, family feuds, prejudices, and all the other life experiences that bring messiness and turmoil. No wonder the arid sands of the Sahara are called desert. When we experience alienation and find ourselves in the wilderness we can feel very deserted.

OUR SPIRITUAL QUEST

Catholic spirituality is about journeying through the wilderness on our way home to the promised land. For centuries, Catholic prayer has symbolized our spiritual quest as a journey by means of processions and pilgrimages. At the shrine of Lourdes, the sick, the maimed, the invalid are wheeled through the night, their path illuminated by flickering candles of hope. The destination of their desert pilgrimage is life-giving water. The invalids are dipped into the flowing spring water with a prayer that they return to health or at least to a revival of hope.

This dynamic is repeated in a small way every time we make a pilgrimage to a parish church. We dip our hand into the holy water and are reminded that we have come in from the dusty road. We can feel again our baptismal energy that flows from living water.

DEEP WATER

When the pioneers first reached the plains of the midwest, they called it the Great American Desert! They did not realize that the mountain streams and spring rains soaked very deep below this desert into the great Ogalala Aquifer, a vast and deep wellspring of life-giving water. The spiritual dimension of our life stories is similar. Beneath the arid cracks in our lives, there is the wellspring of the Spirit. Deep down in our lives dwells the consolation of the Spirit. Isaiah assures us that in the midst of desolation the Spirit can be poured out.

PRAYER TO THE CONSOLING SPIRIT

For the palace will be forsaken,
*   the populous city deserted;*
the hill and the watchtower
*   will become dens forever,*
the joy of wild asses,
*   a pasture for flocks;*
until a spirit from on high is
*   poured out on us,*
*   and the wilderness becomes a*
*   fruitful field*

(Is 32:14–15)

When I feel like an abandoned well,
when I am hollow,
deserted,
disconsolate,
Holy Spirit,
deepest Wellspring—
flowing beneath my tribulations,
break through hard packed sorrows,
Become a fountain of consolation,
springing up to life!

WILLIAM JOHN FITZGERALD

THE EUCHARISTIC ASSEMBLY

After blessing ourselves with holy water, we come home again to the assembly of believers. This reunion at every mass is a return to holy communion and to the communion of saints. But the communion of saints is really a motley and messy crew—even the best of them! It has been so since the beginning. Paul, when he was Saul, stood by approving the stoning of Saint Stephen. Jesus reached out to Paul in his most sinful moment. Peter, the first pope, denied the Lord and ran away, only later to weep bitter tears of remorse. It was precisely at their weakest and most alienated moments that the spirit of Jesus was most at work!

REFLECTION PAUSE

How do you see tears—as a weakness or as a blessing?

Have you held them back? Do you need the Lord to touch you in the midst of tears?

EVERY MASS—A WOUNDED ASSEMBLY

Every eucharistic assembly is the same—so many folks there who experience messiness of one kind or another. So many are present who experience loss, separation, and anguish. As a pastor, I know that I am a wounded healer gathering together other wounded ones but it is precisely in their messy woundedness that amazing grace thrives.

As I look out this morning at the 8:00 A.M. mass, I see Ed, 96 years old, widowed for seven years. He walks to mass every morning. He joins us for coffee after mass. He will sing a song at the drop of a hat. He is cheerful and full of stories. He has passed through grief and the loss of his wife and most of his friends down through the years. Yet, he is a walking icon of cheerful hope.

I see Ron, in mid-life, a victim of downsizing. Since being let go, he has tried many jobs. A white collar business type, he even took a job as a bank guard and learned to shoot and carry a gun. The job didn't fit, but he was willing to submit to it in order to provide for his family.

At the coffee after mass, I sit next to an uncle who had to go to a suburban home and identify the body of his niece who had been raped and killed by two teenagers. And I hear this uncle speak against the "vengeance of the death penalty." I am humbled by such a radical response to the gospel. I marvel and wonder if I could ever imitate his attitude. He would seem to have every right to be vengeful yet the Spirit seems to have moved him in a totally different direction.

I see two parents who suffered the tragic loss of their twelve-year-old son. I see others on medication for emotional wounds. These are members of the homecoming crowd—alumni and alumnae in the fraternity of pain, the sorority of sorrow.

Reflection Pause

When you sit side by side with other folks who appear to have their lives together, do you ever recognize that they have their messy family closets too—that messiness is a given?

What is your messiness now? Who is joined to you in the fraternity of pain, the sorority of sorrow? Are you prayerful about others around who may bear even greater pain? Can you bring some to mind? Be one with them in compassion?

We are not alone in the universe; rather, we are one with the cosmos in the great mystery of tribulation and chaos. Our belief in the Spirit assures us that this cosmic turbulence has an ultimate gentle and guiding hand that is gracious.

PRAYER TO THE UNIFYING SPIRIT

Where can I go from your spirit?
  Or where can I flee from your
    presence?
If I ascend to heaven, you are
    there;
  if I make my bed in Sheol,
    you are there.
If I take the wings of the
    morning
  and settle at the farthest limits
    of the sea,
even there your hand shall lead
    me,
and your right hand shall hold
    me fast.

(Ps 139:7–10)

The stars that scatter across the sky—seemingly apart,
  isolated like broken pieces of light
    are really one.
The Divine energy that hurled them into galaxies
  surges beneath their molecules—
    and mine!
Their luster flickers, dims, and brightens again.
  Passing clouds shall not put out their light,
    nor mine!
All who suffer have a place in this universe, on this
    earth, under the stars.
  in the palm of God's hand.

WILLIAM JOHN FITZGERALD

Coming home to find spirituality through our messy stories means finding the Spirit in the very depths of pain and discovering life-giving waters beneath the desert wastelands in our lives. Such a homecoming joins us to all the others experiencing messiness.

This homecoming means even more. It means creating something new from messiness, even if it is only the spark of hope and a flame of love. There is no new human creation, no new beauty that has not come from the messiness of an artist's palette, the messy process of birth, or the mysterious darkness of our imaginations.

Necessarily, much of our life story is played out at a surface level. On so many days we function out of habit and routine. However, deep down within us there is the potential for creativity. What is deepest below our surface activity is the God-given capacity to change our old patterns, to create something new for ourselves, for others and for God. This is a mysterious gift of the Spirit. Amazingly, it may even lay shrouded in the dregs of some of our most messy human experience. Sometimes we have to plunge into the depths to salvage the sunken treasure to be found in our life stories and fashion it anew.

PRAYER TO THE CREATIVE SPIRIT

Save me, O God,
for the waters have come up
to my neck.
I sink in deep mire,
where there is no foothold;
I have come into deep waters,
and the flood sweeps over me.

(Ps 69:1–2)

Holy Spirit, Unifier, Consoler,
Source of creativity,
Great Diver plumbing our depths,
Salvage the sunken pieces of our lives and dreams.
Bring forth hidden treasure from our muddy stories.
Launch a new ship into the vortex of chaos.
Raise up my spirit from scuttled hopes.
From the murky depths,
Christen my journey to a safe harbor.

WILLIAM JOHN FITZGERALD

IMAGES FOR OUR DAY

We can look back into our personal life stories and find the consoling, unifying, and creative Spirit at work. We can also search for other images that suggest the workings of the Spirit. In former ages, stained glass windows put us in touch with the Spirit infused communion of saints. Today, video images flood our psyches. Using our imaginations, I believe we can even connect some of the video images of our day with the age-old icons of the saints!

"CHEERS!"

Cheers, for many people, is a well known television show. This sitcom set in a Boston bar "where everybody knows your name" is now syndicated, and as a television classic will likely be shown for many years. When I think of the messy characters on *Cheers*, I'm reminded that as messed up as they are, they are pretty similar in their flawed personas not only to myself, but to a lot of people I know. They also remind me of some of our great saints at some stages in their lives!

Saint Augustine, who ran around in his youth and fathered a child out of wedlock, would understand Sam, the playboy bartender on *Cheers*. There are other resemblances. Cliff, the mailman, always struggling to find his way, reminds me of the little guy Zacchaeus hanging out on the tree limb, too insignificant and too small to be a regular member of the crowd.

Carla, the nasty and intemperate barmaid would be quite at home with Saint Jerome, one of the most cantankerous of all the saints. Diane, manipulative and neurotic, reminds me of the Samaritan woman at the well who changed the subject and tried to con Jesus.

Pompous Frasier brings to mind the disciples who wanted the first place in the Kingdom. Norm Peterson, the underachiever, is the mildly alienated everyman of American culture, away from home (where he belongs), trying to fill the hunger of his soul with beer. He is pretty skeptical about life in general—like the doubting apostle Thomas.

Rebecca, the climber, always clawing her way to the top of the corporate ladder, is like the mother of the sons of Zebedee, scheming to achieve places of power.

MESSY MATERIALS
It is precisely the skeptical Norms and the doubting Thomases, the horny Sams and Augustines, the overachieving Baby Boomer Rebeccas and ambitious mother of Zebedee who provide the messiness that the Spirit loves! Their muddied life experiences provide the raw material for saints!

The image of saint-making that the scriptures provide is not one of God shaping His holy ones—like a baker using cookie cutters. Isaiah tells us God is not a cookie cutter, rather, our God is a potter patiently shaping messy clay, making something new and beautiful out of mud!

> *Yet, O LORD, You are our*
> *Father;*
> *we are the clay, and You are*
> *our potter;*
> *we are all the work of Your*
> *hand.*

(Is 64:8)

THE MESSY JOURNEY OF LOVING

All of these *Cheers* characters have feet of clay. So do I. So do you. Like them, we belong to a bedraggled procession struggling toward that safe home where everyone will know our name, and where all depend on all. On our journey, the Spirit does not disdain our turmoil. Our greatest weakness, our deepest alienation, our most profound sorrow may provide the gap where love can grow.

Just as the farmer breaks the hard soil and plants the seed in the deepest furrow—it is in the breaking points of our lives that the dynamic Spirit wants to break through.

REFLECTION PAUSE

Where is the deepest furrow in your life now? Where is the deepest furrow in the lives of your loved ones? Imagine your life as a newly plowed field and invite the Spirit of God to plant something new there.

THE LOST AND FOUND

Belonging to church ought to mean that we belong to one great lost and found department. When Billy at the swimming pool gate, or Sam at the bar, or any of the messy folks who gather for eucharist are most lost—they may be closest to being found.

When we allow the Spirit of God to break into our messy stories, the Spirit can unite us with all who suffer, bring consolation to our aching hearts, and even give creative energy for a better day ahead. The Spirit can stir up compassion for all the wounded we see around us. We are no longer like Billy at the swimming pool gate, deserted and alone. Our very messiness can be the raw material of love, the earthy seedbed for new growth, the muddy garden path that leads us home.

LITANY OF ALIENATION

The abused...	Lord have mercy.
The divorced...	Christ have mercy.
The homeless...	Lord have mercy.
Women put down at work...	Mary of Magdala, pray for them.
Women alienated in the church...	Mary, confidante of Jesus, speak for them.
Aliens without green cards...	Holy Family in Egypt, welcome them.
The unemployed...	Saint Joseph, the worker, help them.
The displaced...	Saint Anthony, find them.
The money laden...	Saint Francis, free them.
The hypnotized consumers...	Saint Joan of Arc, lift their siege.
The old...	May we listen to their wisdom.
The widowed...	May we companion their journey.
Gays...	May we accept their dignity.
Prophets...	May we engage their challenge.
Men with father wounds...	Heal their hearts.
Walled out minorities...	Bridge their troubled waters.
Walled in suburbanites...	Bridge their isolation.
Running yuppies...	Slow them down.
Graying babyboomers...	Mellow their dreams.
Numbed workers...	Allow their creativity.
Disillusioned reformers...	Lift their spirits.
Star warriors...	Give them a better vision.
The sick...	Heal them.
The handicapped...	May we know their giftedness.
Children in the womb...	Let them be.
The children...	Affirm their worth.
The teens...	Give them hope.
The addicted...	Show them twelve steps.
Sisters and brothers...	Spare them from favoritism.

Adult children…	*Deliver them from shame.*
Students…	*Unlock wisdom.*
Those left out…	*Let them in.*
All of us who limp…	*Lord have mercy.*
All of us who cry…	*Christ have mercy.*
All of us who grieve…	*Lord have mercy.*
All of us who are alienated…	*Christ have mercy.*
All of us who are sometimes lost…	*Bring us home through our messy stories.*

WILLIAM JOHN FITZGERALD

PERSONAL REFLECTION—ON THE LITANY OF ALIENATION

Sometimes you yourself will fit in the Litany of Alienation. At all times some of your friends and loved ones will. You might pray the litany, inserting appropriate names in the dotted spaces.

1. *The petition in the Litany of Alienation that most moved me to prayer was…………….*

2. *A childhood memory of my own, similar to Billy's rejection was…………….*

3. *Even today, I sometimes replay that painful experience when I…………….*

4. *I pray to the consoling, unifying, and creative Spirit that…………….*

SCRIPTURE REFLECTIONS—

I could pray on days when I feel like:
   Sam—not quite able to get all the rooms in order: (Jn 14:1–12)
   Diane—uptight from trying to get all the rooms in order: (Mt 6: 24–34)
   Norm—apathetic and stuck: (Heb 12:11–13)
   Rebecca—tired from pushing and afraid of falling: (Heb 12:1–6)
   Cliff—left out, ignored, trying to get in: (Lk 19:1–10)

2

Homecoming Stories of Chaos and Spirit Companions

Dance, dance wherever you may be!
I am the Lord of the dance said he! [5]

In His thirty-three years of life on this earth, Jesus passed through the messiness of daily life, but He endured the chaos of crucifixion for just three hours within one day. He spent three days, no more, in the tomb. That was more than enough. He was then ready to dance the resurrection dance! Chaos demands movement. If you are going through hell, don't stop!

In the classic movie, *Zorba The Greek*, after the rope of their scaffold is cut and the two heroes' business venture collapses in dust, Zorba proclaims, "A man needs a little madness, or he never dares to cut the rope and be free!" Then his friend proclaims, "Teach me to dance!" Arm in arm, laughing, they enter into a wild spirited Greek dance. [6]

We cannot endure interminable chaos. We have to get up and move, join the dance. The dance is a configuration of chaos, a gathering together of swirling energies. In the dance, the wild and confusing motions come together into a flow. Chaos can often be transformed into creative energy.

MYTHS AND METAPHORS

We need stories, images, myths, and metaphors similar to the Zorba story to encourage us that there are ways to move through chaos and come home again to the Spirit who sustains us. We must cope with messiness. We must move out of chaos. One woman's story illustrates this need to keep moving. A Scottsdale resident started taking a lot of medication for chronic stiff muscles—the result of one hellish year in which her business failed, she got a divorce, her house foreclosed, her dog died, and her car blew up!

Her story is more than messy; it is chaotic. When interviewed, she went on to state that she was taking new action beyond the pills, seeking counsel and beginning alternative therapy. She was not about to linger in chaos. When chaos erupts new energies can stir up from its swirling confusion. Spirited companions may help us move forward to write a better story.

A FOOTBALL METAPHOR

On New Year's Eve, 1988, the night before Notre Dame played for the national championship in the Fiesta Bowl, I gave an Evening of Recollection at a retreat center on "The Spirituality of Football—The Notre Dame Myth." Twenty people attended, nineteen women and one man. They did not know the topic until they arrived. When I announced it, some eyes rolled, some feet shuffled and a few faces frowned. It was obvious that they were not captivated by the topic. However, I was not proposing football as a spiritual tonic, but I was suggesting that its imagery parallels messiness and chaos. Moreover, the Notre Dame football myth proclaims a passage through chaos, sometimes against great odds.

I shared with them how moving through messiness and chaos with spirited companions is vividly exemplified by the football metaphor. The game is among the messiest of all sports, often played in the mud. The ballcarrier must move through swirling chaos aided by spirited companions. The ball can get muddy and takes unexpected twists and turns, not always bouncing your way. Sometimes you drop it and sometimes you catch it. Football mirrors our human inability to always be in control.

In football when you are knocked down, you have to get up and try again. This image of moving through chaos is very applicable to our real life stories. When we find ourselves victims of grief, loss, or rejection, a mourning period is essential; but eventually, often in stages, we must move out of chaos. For the many victims of domestic violence in our society, staying put could mean being trampled to death by chaos.

ORGANIZED CHAOS

I concluded my talk to my initially skeptical listeners by stressing that our games mirror for us the need to grab the ball and run. For a visitor watching football for the first time, it seems like an explosion of twisting, turning, confused bodies. It resembles nothing more than a confused disorderly mass. Yet, it is a complex game of organized chaos. Sometimes there are surprising victories and homecomings.

The game is not always fair; you sometimes get penalized when you don't deserve it. The goal—after all the sweat and chaos, the ups and downs, the penalties, and the yards gained—is to come home with a victory. And if the ball bounces the wrong way or the referee's call is unfair, and defeat occurs in this particular game, the homecoming is bitter. On the other hand, the game film can be studied, for there are lessons to be learned in reflecting on defeat. There will be another game, and another chance to win and someday a better homecoming.

I also talked to them about the Notre Dame football myth. At the end of my presentation about football mirroring life, the nineteen ladies smiled, nodded their heads and admitted, yes, football is a pretty good metaphor for the messiness and chaos we experience in our life journeys. When they shared some of the turmoil experienced in marriage and in widowhood as well as their worries about business downsizing and what the future might hold, the images from football of winning and losing, being knocked down and getting up again, and the support that can come from teamwork became more vivid and helped them to focus on the need to cope with messiness and move through chaos.

A WINNING MYTH

The day after I gave that talk about football as a metaphor for chaos in our lives, I sat in the Fiesta Bowl watching Notre Dame play for the national championship. As I listened to the famous Notre Dame Victory March—"Shake down the thunder from the skies…old Notre Dame will win over all," I was immersed once more in the Notre Dame football myth. It too is about moving out of chaos with spirited companions.

OUR LADY AND THE IMMIGRANTS' DREAM

Most of us who are descendants of immigrants or slaves should be able to relate to the Notre Dame myth, for part of it is about immigrants moving out of turmoil against great odds and writing a new homecoming story. When Catholic immigrants left the "old country," they escaped from chaos. And when they arrived in their new land, they were not always welcomed by the white, Anglo-Saxon-Protestant establishment.

There were two ladies, however, who did reach out to the "refuse" from foreign shores. One was Lady Liberty. The other was Our Lady—Notre Dame atop a golden dome in South Bend, Indiana. No wonder the Notre Dame Fighting Irish became the immigrants' team and gained thousands of subway alumni supporters across the country. This little school coached by Knute Rockne, an immigrant's son, made a home for newcomers with strange names. KNUTE, ARA Parseghian, ANGELO Bertelli, ZYGMONT Czrobski, RAGHIB, "Rocket" Ismail were names of Notre Dame heroes that outsiders and underdogs could identify with. The Notre Dame football myth is about the children of immigrants and slaves, moving up out of chaos—underdogs claiming a new home. It is about them joining together as spirit companions and writing new stories, "though the odds be great or small," as the famous Notre Dame Victory March proclaims.

THE MYTH LIVES ON

That day at the Fiesta Bowl, Notre Dame won the national championship. Lou Holtz, its coach, whose desire as a young man to attend Notre Dame was dashed by an admission rejection, came home to his youthful dream. Once locked out, he now was carried into the Notre Dame locker room on the shoulders of his players. Having beaten the odds of a chaotic early life rejection, he was now a Notre Dame man after all.

Notre Dame football does provide powerful metaphors for moving through chaos with spirit companions. Years later, I would meet Lou Holtz, and he talked about the need to "pick yourself up and go" when you are in the midst of chaos.

(Overlooking the Notre Dame football stadium, a giant mural of Jesus, with arms uplifted, has been nicknamed Touchdown Jesus by the Notre Dame students.)

PRAYER TO TOUCHDOWN JESUS

Jesus, with outstretched arms and smiling face,
help me to thread my way through a broken field.
  If I am out of bounds,
    show me the way back again.

When I miss a pass,
deliver me from passing the buck.
  Give me the energy
    to turn "Wish Bone" to backbone,

> *fumble to recovery,*
> *loss to gain,*
> *defeat to victory.*

> *With spirit companions,*
> *may I beat the odds,*
> *though great or small,*
> *and come home again*
> *to where I belong,*
> *next to the golden lady*
> *at Your side.*

WILLIAM JOHN FITZGERALD

WE SOMETIMES LOSE

But Notre Dame does NOT win all the time, nor do we. Sometimes, when we have done everything right, we fall short, or cataclysmic events intervene. Making choices and just living is risky. Chaos can disrupt our lives. We all risk loss and failure. When this occurs, we need to MOVE THROUGH chaos—not accepting it as a permanent state. Each day, through the media, we are bombarded with images of chaos. They often exceed images of kindness, recovery, forgiveness, joy, creativity and hope. We can run the risk of succumbing—of becoming convinced that our world is basically chaotic, mean and dangerous. As a result we can get stuck in fear, passivity, or cynicism. We need metaphors and images of hope. We also need to observe real life persons recovering from chaos. As a pastor I have a box seat.

THE CHAOS OF SEPARATION, LOSS, GRIEF

That New Year's day at the Fiesta Bowl, I watched a game that is a metaphor for chaos. From my vantage point as a pastor I observe much more. I encounter the real stories of chaos and spirit companions; they can be even more dramatic and hope-filled than any game.

Many of my parishioners are single parents. As this is written, nationally one third of all parents are single parents. For so many of these there are no time outs. The pace is hectic. The game-clock is always running, and they are one coach short. However, many grow beyond the chaos of separation and perform admirably under great pressure.

Loss and the resulting grief can be chaotic. I have so many pastoral memories of standing with shocked survivors next to a lake that had trapped a loved one in drowning grip, or standing beside body bags—plastic shrouds containing charred remains. I have stood in fetid sick-rooms beside grieving parents, and traced the holy oils on the black-pocked foreheads of sons with AIDS who have come home to die. The journey of bereavement from such chaos can never be measured.

Two of my former students have been murdered. Recently, a son of a parishioner was severely beaten and left on a doorstep to die. Neither they nor their survivors did anything to deserve this kind of chaos. When such tragedies occur, words fail. One can only stand in solidarity—a spirit companion to the survivors as they inch their way through their own inner chaos. (A profile of a spirit companion is highlighted at the end of this chapter.)

LOCKED IN BY CHAOS

Recently, I also had the opportunity of meeting and visiting with Terry Anderson, who moved through chaos with hope and grace. Whereas Lou Holtz was *locked out* of his boyhood dream, Terry was *locked in* to extreme chaos as a hostage in Lebanon. Terry Anderson spent seven years as a hostage in chained captivity. Yet he said that, in Beirut, that hell-hole of violent hate, for every person he encountered with evil intent, he met hundreds of other good and caring people. His story testifies to the endurance of the human spirit and the ability to keep moving even in confinement, when chaos is senseless and long enduring. One of the lessons he took from his long imprisonment was that the human spirit is extremely difficult to crush. Terry described himself and his fellow captives as ordinary people facing extraordinary tests. He said his experience raised his consciousness—we human beings are capable of far more than we think possible. He went on to say, "I now believe that pain, change, and growth are connected. We were forced to reach within to discover what we were really capable of." [7]

Even though Terry and the other hostages were sometimes taped up like mummies and shuffled from one hideout to another, were abused and kept in the dark, the spark of their inner spirits kept leaping up from their abyss.

When I think of the hostages' imprisonment, I am reminded of other types of confinement that exist in every community. In my parish, Milt was an engaging fellow, a good athlete, a golf pro with many friends. In his last years, he sat in a care center and rocked, isolated from all that he knew by the prison walls of Alzheimer's disease. His wife Therese and his family kept vigil and were faithful until the Lord released that inner spark at the core of his being which not even Alzheimer's could quench. Therese's faith assures her that Milt can come home again now that his soul has broken free into eternal life.

In my pastoral experience, I have also known Mary, a widow who is blind. Because she was raised as an orphan and started working at an early age, she never received her high school diploma. After raising a fine family and working hard all her life, at the age of 93, this valiant woman studied from tape recordings and received her GED diploma!

IMAGES FOR MOVING THROUGH CHAOS

The stories of Terry Anderson and the other hostages in Lebanon, as well as the lives of Therese and Mary and other vigil keepers, and their companionship in the school of suffering provide real life images of endurance outlasting chaos. Terry Anderson came home to spirituality through his messy hostage story. He also came home to a six-and-one-half-year-old daughter he had never met. We need homecoming images like his to help us hope through our own chaos no matter what the odds.

Saint Paul, who experienced the chaos of sudden blindness, ship-wreck, and floggings, wrote about hopeful endurance and used the sweaty race as an image for the struggles that are part of our spiritual stories.

Therefore, since we are surrounded by so great a cloud of witnesses, let us also lay aside every weight and the sin that clings so closely, and let us run with perseverance the race that is set before us,.... (Heb 12:1)

In a race, you keep moving. If Paul were with us today he might use a football image to write a homecoming story that moves through and beyond chaos.

ENDURANCE

When Terry Anderson visited us, he was very moved when he met a frail Vietnamese who was once an army officer in Vietnam. Life has not been fair to him either. The chaos of war crashed into his life. An exile, he now works in custodial service far from his birthplace. When asked how he survived thirteen years of imprisonment in chains, he replied, "Meditation—I went inside myself into a better world." His coping with imprisonment illustrates again that the sustaining and consoling Spirit can be found even at the very vortex of chaos. His too is a homecoming story of freedom against all odds.

REFLECTION PAUSE

Do you know anyone experiencing such chaos? Bring the person daily to prayer. Stand with the person, not saying, "I know how you feel!" because you can't; but rather let the person know that you simply stand WITH THEM.

Consider in your own life lesser experiences of chaos: Can the bad bounces in your own life be turned around? Do you see bad bounces as victimizations or challenges?

What may need to be done to move out of chaos and come home to peace and freedom? Can you tell the difference between messiness and chaos in your life?

What kind of help do you need from the Lord if you are moving through the chaos of bereavement?

Have you talked to your funeral director about finding a grief support group?

Bring the risen Jesus to mind. Let Him take your hand and lead you away from the tomb. Journal or talk to Him about how chaos feels. Ask Him to lead you through.

PRAYER FOR THOSE IN CHAOS

He bowed the heavens, and
*   came down;*
thick darkness was under his
*   feet.*

He reached down from on high,
*   he took me;*
he drew me out of mighty
*   waters.*

(Ps 18:9 & 16)

From depths of tears and chaos,
Holy Spirit, seize us.
raise us from the murky deep—
out of swirling and choking waters.

Emerge from the cyclonic center
of our inner chaos.

Deliver us from the eye of the storm.
Energy of the Spirit, move us.

I pray for myself and those I love
who linger in chaos.
Consoling Spirit hover near cold tombs.
Fire of the Spirit, warm us.

When we are bogged down,
and tomorrow seems a dark dream,
Spirit-Wind, rattle our windows.
Lightning-Spirit, awaken us.

Stir us from inertia,
fear and cynicism.
Change "Life is not fair!"
to "We can and will move on!"

WILLIAM JOHN FITZGERALD

MOVING ON

Moving forward for some people, like Terry Anderson and his companions, and those we know who are sick, paralyzed, elderly may mean only an inner movement of the heart and spirit—living into the next day. Hope is a leap of the inner spirit. It is the dimension in our stories that opens new chapters. Hope is a cutting of the rope that binds our soul. Faith pushes us forward. Hope pulls us through.

To stay put in permanent chaos means self-destruction. There are many patterns of self-destruction. All the denials that accompany various addictions and domestic abuse are invitations to chaos. Sometimes, for some suicidal persons, no movement is seen as possible. They perceive themselves as stuck. But chaos ought to wake us up rather than put us to sleep.

We need to dance in the midst of chaos as Zorba did. For Terry Anderson and his companions and for the many others we see locked in, the dance may only be of the inner spirit. But their example can encourage us to turn chaotic chapters of our life stories toward the ultimate direction of resurrection.

REFLECTION PAUSE

Reflect for a few moments. Think of the Zorba figures in your own life, people who express hope against great odds, and who energize you for the journey ahead. Bring them to mind; thank God for them.

Do you know any wounded or homebound people who seem bound, but whose inner spirits are free? Pray for the hope-inspired movement needed in your own life.

Recall for a few moments the courageous homecoming stories of your own ancestors. Bask a little in their courage and hope.

CHAOS TELLS US TO MOVE!

Chaos can be the preface to a new chapter in our life stories. For Jesus, the most chaotic Good Friday chapter was closest to the most glorious chapter entitled *Resurrection!* and His coming home to the Father. Some chaos is unavoidable. Whether it turns into creative energy or destruction is often for us to choose. The pain of alienation can also unleash either our bitterness or our compassion. Compassion born of alienation has creative power.

Being locked out or locked in can be chaotic at any age. At age fifty, during Holy Week, I agonized over my perception of being shunned as a pastor by a significant group of parishioners. On Holy Thursday night, rejection seemed to envelop me like a shroud. The memory of this adult experience of the dark is much more painful than the childhood memory of being locked out at the swimming pool gate.

I was newly assigned as a pastor of the largest parish in the city, eager to write a new chapter in my life. Before I could really get to know anyone or be known, a series of events occurred that caused great conflict. A group in the parish felt that I was not behind them. When I needed welcome, I perceived a growing sense of rejection leading into alienation. It finally led into clinical depression. I knew chaos. At that moment, I made the right decision. I made a move out of inertia. I got into psychological counseling, began taking medication and sought spiritual direction. One advisor said, "As pastor, you appear official, very secure, self-confident to your people. They have no sense of your woundedness. You have good friends outside the parish who really know you and know your real story, but no one among your parishioners knows. It is essential for you to find a few spirit companions with whom you can journey on this new venture. Let them be people who can hear your deeper story, experience your messiness, share your pain. Be at home with them. Be sure they are folks you can also laugh with. Find them, and you will no longer be an alien, a shepherd in the mist."

I did find them. Months later, on Holy Thursday, I found myself heavily burdened with depression. I remembered a scene from the Holy Land where we were shown a pit where prisoners were sometimes held awaiting trial. The guide had remarked that it was possible that on the first Holy Thursday, Jesus may have been lowered into that pit during the deliberations concerning His fate. That image of the deep pit, a vision of utter chaos, filled my imagination, I felt that I was in that pit on Holy Thursday. I knew I could not remain there. I called several of my new friends in the parish and they were all out of town. I finally reached a married woman who was one of my new friends. That night, after I appeared so all together at the Holy Thursday liturgy, I told her what it felt like to be lowered into that pit. She listened. She did not say, "You should not feel that way." She did not try to rescue me. Instead, she responded, "You must know that you are not alone. Your other friends and I are with you. You are loved by us and will be by this parish. We'll be with you on your journey…maybe you need a hug…but better, I think…that I hold you in my praying heart."

When my friend went out the door, I closed the door on this bitter and depressed chapter of my life. The enveloping depression lifted like a fleeing fog, not to return. That messy moment of crisis opened into something new and healing. The very moment when I experienced the worst of chaos, I was closest to resurrection.

BEING LIFTED FROM CHAOS TO VICTORY

We are fortunate if an energetic and forward moving spirited companion like my friend in the parish gives us a wake-up call to chaos, or if we are alerted to its presence by an intervention at work or even by illness. An addiction or an illness can bring us to the depth of chaos—which is really at the edge of resurrection—if we can only move beyond the edge; if we don't stay stuck. However, we can poison our own inner spiritual wells by being surrounded by acquaintances who deny our pain, and not by spirit companions— soul friends—who engage our deepest hearts. As Ed Sellner reminds us in his book, *Mentoring*, a person bereft of a soul friend resembles a limy well without any refreshing water.

CHAOS OR MESSINESS?

If there has been no intervention in our life that demands a recognition of our own chaos, how do we know the difference between messiness and chaos? The bottom line is that unrelenting chaos is deadly while messiness is uncomfortable. We move out of chaos. We cope with messiness. Any move out of chaos is a victory over dissolution. In order to recognize chaos in our own life, we need to look around at the stories of others. Alcoholism and the other addictions left untreated are ultimately fatal. Untreated depression can be. So can unrelieved stress and a poisoned environment. Observe the corroding patterns in the life stories of others that result in disintegration. We need to read the signs that are all around us, and not exempt ourselves from scrutiny.

Tragic loss of loved ones is chaotic, but we can observe in the lives of others that time begins to heal such wounds. The same can be true for other losses we might experience.

REFLECTION PAUSE

Take a few moments and observe some of the famous people and celebrities who have gone before us. Some have died from accidents and unavoidable illnesses. There are some, though, who might still be enlivening our lives by their presence. Were there destructive patterns in their lives that went untreated?

If you could stand outside as an observer and examine your own lifestyle would you find any similar patterns? If your IMMEDIATE answer is the denial of "Not me!"—take another prayerful look.

Does the very question confuse you? Then look again.

DISCERNMENT

Chaos is like a whirling dust storm that can leave us confused and not knowing which way to turn. William Barry, S.J., in his book *Paying Attention to God*, gives some hints about discerning our way through confusion. Regarding important life career choices, he indicates that a key question to ask when discerning a better way to go is this: Which path seems to offer a challenge which can lead to fulfillment and satisfaction? This is the way that the Spirit would lead us.

However this question cannot usually be pondered if we are immersed in chaos. But it can and should be asked when a tempest has quieted and we search for a way through the resulting messiness. But what if chaos is unrelenting? It remains challenging but it can never be satisfying or fulfilling. It becomes a self-chosen prison.

Barry goes on to say that any activity or pattern in our life which closes us into ourselves and makes us more fearful is not the way of the consoling and energizing Spirit.

In order to become more discerning, we need practice in prayerful attention to the movements of our hearts, prayerful reflection on them, and honest appraisal of what seems more in tune with God's one action. What leads to greater faith, hope, and love in our hearts? What seems more likely to enhance communion and community among those with whom we live and work? [8]

Ultimately, discernment means knowing the difference between chaos and ordinary messiness. It means finding a Spirit-led way out of chaos and a Spirit-inspired way to cope with messiness as we move toward the fulfillment that is the fruit of the Spirit.

SPIRIT COMPANIONS—SOUL FRIENDS

We need spirit companions who can help us discern the difference between ordinary messiness and relentless chaos. When passing through the worst of chaos and trying to live with messiness, spirit companions who will hold us in their praying hearts are priceless treasures. What do spirit companions look like? Like my wise friend. Like the dancing Zorba who keeps moving. Like Terry Anderson and his chained companions. Like football teammates who exude energy even when they are behind in the game and the clock is running. They look like married couples who experience inevitable conflict and turbulence, but who pay attention to each other's pain, who tell each other, "Here's what I am feeling, let's talk about it…I am not going to complain about you to someone else— you are my companion; listen to my pain, and I will listen to yours and then let's do something about it."

They can look like the members of small faith sharing communities in my parish, and in many other places, who listen to each other in an atmosphere of faith and hope. They can be recognized. They radiate hope. They share their stories. They move through chaos together. They may help each other to write new homecoming stories.

A CHECKLIST FOR A SPIRIT COMPANION

✦ Could you be one? Do you need one? Do you know a friend who needs one?

✦ Someone who has experienced their own alienation which has schooled them in compassion.

✦ Someone who has fumbled the ball but has picked it up again and has continued the zigzag run toward the end zone.

✦ A journeyer, wise enough to know that to journey is to be still on the way.

✦ One who can laugh at personal foibles, realizing that we are all characters.

✦ At home with self, not co-dependent.

✦ With a Bible in the back-pack, for nourishment, not for quick fix solutions.

✦ One who leans forward trying to catch all the sounds of your voice and your heart.

✦ One who looks more like a hiker than a judge, a parent, or a coach.

✦ One who has Zorba's zest for life and deep belief that obstacles are hurdles to be leaped, not dead end blockades.

✦ A hiker who travels light with no rescue equipment on hand.

✦ Someone wise enough to show you the compass direction to professional help if that is what you need, and courageous enough to advise it.

✦ Someone who can live through paradox and contradictions.

✦ Someone with more good questions than quick answers.

✦ Someone who believes and prays and holds you in their praying heart.

✦ Someone who walks with you as you search for the well-spring of your own heart.

✦ Someone who can be a friend to your soul—your deeper self.

✦ Someone who knows from hard experience that sometimes we

will only discover life's golden treasures by venturing into turbulent streams and dark caves.

✦ Someone who knows that the way you pan for gold on your journey is to sift through the grit and gravel of messy human experience.

✦ Someone who has a feel for the trail leading home.

PERSONAL REFLECTION—WHERE ARE YOU IN THE MESSINESS, CHAOS, SPIRIT COMPANION GAME?

How do you feel?

I feel the need to take time out.

I am feeling the emptiness of a loss.

I feel like trying to make a comeback.

I feel like the air is out of my football.

I feel like celebrating a victory.

Why?

Do I need to cope with messiness or make a move out of chaos?

Review the checklist of a spirit companion. Who do I know who might fit that description? Could one of them help me discern about questions of messiness or chaos?

SCRIPTURE REFLECTIONS

Acts 2:1–21	THE HUDDLING DISCIPLES ENLIVENED BY THE SPIRIT.
Lk 9:57–60	DISCIPLESHIP DEMANDS MOVEMENT.
Lk 12: 35–38	SEIZE THE MOMENT TO ACT AND RESPOND.
1 Thes 5:6–11	DELIVERANCE FROM CHAOS WITH SPIRIT COMPANIONS.
Rom 8:26–39	THE SPIRIT IN THE MIDST OF HARDSHIPS.

3

Coming Home to Our Children Through the Messy Stable

When I think of messy parenting, a travel memory haunts me. I am aboard Amtrak's Empire Builder somewhere in Montana. I sit in the club car drinking a cola and writing. We are hurtling westward at seventy miles per hour. I am in my grubbies. How did she know I was a priest? "Give me ten minutes, Father"…and then, very loudly, "Two weeks ago, my son hanged himself in the county jail in Saint Paul…Am I to blame?"

For a few moments I found myself speechless, and all that could be heard was the click, click, click of the rail joints as the train put distance between her and tragedy in the Twin Cities. Sometimes parents want out from grief, from guilt, from seemingly unbearable memories. Hers was a journey out of a messy stable.

Sometimes parents want in. Our Lady, who appears so glorious on the Notre Dame golden dome, did not live in a golden home. Like many of our ancestors she was an exile and an immigrant. With her husband Joseph she searched for a place to get in. She wanted the best for her child, but she had to accept messy parenting in a messy place. It has been the same for so many parents down through every age.

Once upon a time, on a dark and holy night, there was an ox, outside where he belonged—in a smelly pasture. There was a donkey who plodded patiently through the night, her breath panting in the frosty air. She too was outside where she belonged. And beyond the city walls there were shepherds and their smelly sheep. They were full-time outsiders—never welcomed in the city.

We've all been outsiders at one time or another, as children unchosen for a team, or perhaps as adults abandoned, widowed, racially segregated, laid off, put down by sexist attitudes, bereaved, sick, a victim of circumstances. It can happen in so many ways. Perhaps one of the more painful outsider experiences is that of parents wanting so much what is good for their children, and feeling locked out.

On that cold and dark night so long ago, there were two young parents locked outside with the ox, the donkey, the sheep, and the shepherds. They were unable to get in anywhere. They wanted a secure place for their child (as all good parents do) but the best they could find for the birthplace of their little one was a cave.

There were others inside, behind locked doors, shuttered hearts, dreamless. They could smell neither the ox nor the donkey moving toward the cave. They could not hear the rustle of the shepherds in the night, or the shuffling of their flocks. They never looked for angels so they never found them. They slept their way through the holy night. And when they got up in the morning and looked out over the city, they never saw the cave at all. It was what we might do with our Hubbel telescope—look far beyond, and miss seeing God very close.

On that holy night, Jesus came into a smelly stable to be God with us. He came into the very midst of our messiness companioned by frightened sheep, a braying donkey, and shepherds who were outsiders. He came as a child to messy parents, tired from their journey, lacking security, not sure of the path ahead. He came at the edge of chaos, for Herod would soon plot His death. Joseph and Mary had to cope with the messiness of the cave, but they would soon have to move out of chaos all the way to Egypt. Spirit companions—three wise persons from the east—would help them to discern a path through messiness and beyond chaos. This nativity scene that the evangelist Luke paints provides a panorama of parental messiness.

PARENTAL ALIENATION
Because parenting is a long and oftentimes messy process, parents and children sometimes stand apart and need to find their way home to each other. As children grow, parents experience the perpetual quandary: "Will they take the right path?" More often than not, at some point they find their offspring in the midst of messiness. Often their children stand on alien ground. The space between can only be bridged by some form of reconciliation. There is also a need for many parents to arrive at an inner peace, letting go of regrets and guilt feelings when they see their offspring travel a road less desired. Often, parents bear false guilt. Too many parents and grandparents hurt too much like the grieving mother on the train in Montana. Too many need a peaceful homecoming for their troubled hearts.

Before Joseph and Mary found Jesus in the temple, they were heartsick and anxious to find Him on a safe path. Their quandary is that of parents through the ages. The eyes of parents and grandparents anxiously scan the horizon. When they reflect on the messy world their children inhabit, they may now realize that dirty diapers were not only the insignia of young parenthood, but they were also the weather flags of days to come.

What are parents and grandparents looking out for? What do they fear along the road ahead for their offspring? Everything from AIDS to zero population, as well as cohabitation, financial insecurity, repeat divorces, spouse abuse, abandonment, the whole addiction catalog, the Bomb, ecological poisoning and birth defects.

They sometimes sense a gulf of alienation and separation. They fear their children will leave home too soon, or not soon enough—that they may never leave home, or that they will move back as single parents and bring their children, or that they will have no grandkids to bring home. They also wonder whether their off-spring will abandon the faith and values of their ancestors and pass a vacuum of faith to their grandkids.

REFLECTION PAUSE

If you are a parent, grandparent or relative, bring to mind family members you worry about. Imagine the messy crib, and place them there in the presence of the smiling infant. Linger with that image.

Despite all these fears, and the perils of modern parenting, young couples and proud grandparents still do as they always have, they look into the eyes of a newborn and their expression seems to say, "Only you and I and God could make such as thee!" Parents of all ages are still in mighty good creative company. Parents can still res-onate with Mary's joyful outcry about parenthood:

> *"My soul magnifies the Lord,*
> *and my spirit rejoices in God*
> *   my Savior…*
> *for the Mighty One has done*
> *   great things for me…*

(Lk 1:47, 49)

Mary would learn, however, that part of the greatness would also be the parental journey through messiness. The crib was sur-rounded by manure. The story of her road to Egypt was the tale of a long and unpleasant journey. Calvary was rain-lashed and muddy. These places and events were part of the alienation journey of Jesus. Beyond this kind of messiness and chaos there was also the best of wine at Cana, the bliss on the Mount of Beatitudes, the healings, and the greetings of peace and reunion in the Easter home of reconciliation. The family experience of Jesus was both hectic and chaotic, as well as joyful and reconciling.

PARENTHOOD TODAY: THE MESSY TENSIONS

Our movies sometimes mirror the parental search for a right path in our own hectic times. In a Feast of the Holy Family homily, I once used illustrations from the film *Parenthood*, an insightful comedy about the messy tensions and glory of child raising and extended family. It probes the joys and struggles of Gil and Karen, their children, and their relatives. These include Gil's parents and brother Larry, as well as two sisters and their families.

The opening scene has Gil and Karen and the kids loading up the car on the way home from the ball game. After all the family paraphernalia is on board and they are out on the highway, nine-year-old Kevin starts to chant: "When you slide into first, and you feel something burst—diarrhea!" [9] When Kevin is asked where he learned this new song and he answers, "At camp!" Dad responds, "Ah, money well spent."

Between that opening scene and the film's warm and beautiful ending there is a lot of messiness. Among the family's dirty laundry list are found:

✦ a recovering alcoholic grandparent,

✦ Helen, a divorced single parent trying to cope with a runaway teenage daughter and a sullen pubescent son angry at his absent father.

✦ another sister who is married to a perfectionist husband who compulsively programs his daughter to be a super high achiever.

✦ Last, but not least, Larry, Gil's brother, the family prodigal who arrives home and presents grandpa and grandma with a new ward named "Cool" and a $26,000 bill owed for gambling debts.

All extended families have some problems. In the film, *Parenthood*, Gil and Karen struggle to cope with their own challenges—from child rearing, school, work, and Little League where nine-year-old Kevin may drop THE all important ball and lose the game. Are these filmed family glitches farfetched? As a pastor, I see many parents waging a daily battle just struggling to keep up with overload and coping as best they can with multiple stressors.

HEROIC VIRTUE

In older spiritual writing, heroic virtue was ascribed to extraordinary tests encountered by the saints. In today's tangled family situations, heroic virtue may well be needed for many in ordinary family life. In his essay, *The Gift of the Good Land,* Wendell Berry writes about two types of heroic quests. Heroes like Samson seize a dramatic moment to perform the heroic deed. More common are the folks involved in the daily messiness of life who persevere in their life tasks with heroic courage. Berry opines that it may be easier to be Samson than to be a good husband or wife day after day for fifty years.

Gil and Karen illustrate the gritty courage needed for such a family quest. When the going gets toughest, and Gil tells off his boss and quits his job because he was passed over for promotion, Karen announces she is pregnant with their fourth child. This dialogue ensues:

Gil: "There's three of them and you want to have four! And the fourth one could be—LARRY! And they're going to do a lot of things….Sometimes they are going to miss!" (catching the fly ball) Karen: "Sometimes, they won't." Gil: "Sometimes they will." Karen: "What do you want me to do, give you guarantees? These are kids, not appliances. Life is messy." Gil: "I hate messy; it's sooo messy!" [10]

In this movie, in almost every scene, the theme of messiness is played out. And then at the end, the camera shows the entire clan gathered at the hospital, some holding infants, and all viewing new-born babies. Despite all their messy family stories, their facial expressions of wonder and rapture show that the new infants have brought them home again to a shared unity and joy. Even though these infant rookies will sooner or later drop the ball, make a mess and make their way through ambiguity, what counts for now is that they belong to a home team.

BELONGING
Belonging to an extended home team becomes more important than ever as the number of single parent families grows. I saw a lot of heads nodding "yes" as I made that point in the homily.

MESSINESS MEANS AMBIGUITY
Spirituality in messiness must come to terms with ambiguity. Who knows the labyrinthian way that led the son of the lady on the train to commit suicide and leave his mother with "if onlys?" How does unrelenting chaos seep into people's lives? Ultimately we must all come to terms with the messiness, chaos, and turmoil of life. For too many, hope evaporates in this process. Suicide is one of the major causes of teen deaths today. Boys Town, a haven for troubled youth, has studied teen suicide. Their literature offers the opinion that over the long run, stopping a teen suicide may depend on being able to coax him or her into coming to terms with life's burdens and con-tradictions.

I remember a lovely twenty-five-year-old who waited for "a

knight in shining armor." A young man even appeared in her driveway on a white horse to woo her. She was beautiful and so highly idealistic. Anorexia wore her down until she could no longer cope with life's contradictions as she perceived them. Like the lady on the train, all who loved her so dearly have had to let go of the "if onlys" and let the gentle Jesus pick up the pieces.

In the case of the most tragic of deaths—suicide, let the gentle Jesus have the last word. He alone can make straight the crooked lines on a suicide note. He alone can decipher the utter silence of an unspoken self-inflicted death.

REFLECTION PAUSE

Are you burdened with "if onlys" about any of your children, grandchildren or dear friends?

Pray for a release from the "if onlys" of the past to be replaced by a hopeful promise of a future reunion.

PARENTAL WORRIES

Parents and grandparents worry about their children and their grandchildren coping with life's slings and arrows. When things go wrong, they may tend to blame themselves. Might it even have been a concern in the Holy Family?

Years after His messy birth in a stable, Jesus would eventually have to experience the chaos of Good Friday. A sword would pierce the heart of His mother and she would have to stand by, helpless, at the foot of the cross. As His life led in the direction of the cross, did she sometimes wonder if He was on the right path? It seems like a good Jewish mother might sometimes ponder and even worry. At the foot of the cross she may have even wondered, "What did I do wrong that He should end up here?"

RECONCILIATION

There are quite a few parents today who feel an alienation, a sense of loss and separation across the generations. Many feel a warp between their values and those of their children. They see the present world moving so fast, they would like to maintain some moorings. The church can be one of their remaining anchors. The church's journey through turbulent times still seems to be guided by some kind of compass that gives a direction toward the Lord. With Peter, they can pray, "…to whom can we go? You have the words of eternal life!" (Jn 6:68)

Many of these parents are at home with being Catholic. Lurking in their imaginations are good childhood memories: midnight masses, May crownings, first communions, the Christmas crib, images of Mary. These images connect them to a heritage being passed down from generation to generation. Their faith still resides in their deepest hearts.

Many of these hearts ache from a perception that this heritage is being abandoned by their children and grandchildren. They see so many dropping out, or on sabbatical from the faith as they understand it. In their hearts, they experience a seeming rejection of what in some sense constitutes their person and familyhood. If there is any truth to "Love me; love my dog," then also there is to "Love me; love our church—or at least "Love *some* church."

More than that, too many parents burden themselves with false guilt. They keep asking themselves, "What did we do wrong? How did we fail?" As a pastor, I agree with an opinion offered by David Hassel, S.J., in his book *Healing the Ache of Alienation:* among good-willed people, the greatest source of alienation from God and from the service of others is false guilt. I once told an assembly of these kinds of parents and grandparents that we should, some afternoon, rent all the football stadiums in the land and invite in all hurting parents and grandparents. Then we should have some wonderful healing and reconciliation service that would release them from all the guilt and pain that they bear for their children's and grandchildren's apparent drift from God. I've never had any remark I have made draw so many nodding heads.

ABSALOM AND DAVID

I got that response when preaching about King David and his estranged son, Absalom. This son, so full of promise, joined a revolt against his father and was killed in battle. Even though Absalom was rebelling, his death broke David's heart.

It was told Joab, "The king is weeping and mourning for Absalom." So the victory that day was turned into mourning for all the troops; for the troops heard that day, "The king is grieving for his son."…The king covered his face, and the king cried with a loud voice, "O my son Absalom, O Absalom, my son, my son!" (2 Sm 19:1–4)

This scripture story touched the listeners because so many parents and grandparents are like the mourning David. Their children or grandchildren seem dead in one way or another. So many older generation figures mourn something that has seemed to die between themselves and some of the members of younger generations. They try to second guess what went wrong in the raising of the younger ones. Their lament is, "What did we do wrong?"

+ Our children are in multiple marriages.

+ Our children live together without marriage.

+ Our children are in no church.

+ Our children are addicted.

+ Our children are estranged.

+ Our children are far away from us in body and in spirit.

+ Our children have turned their backs on their heritage after some of us paid out immense sums for an education that would pass on our heritage.

A PARENT'S LITANY

A great litany might arise from stadiums of discontent and disappointment. If we gathered that chant from all the assemblies, it would fill the heavens with a great sound. It would be a roaring sigh like that of David mourning his lost son Absalom. The reconciliation that would need to happen in the stadiums of discontent would have to be a great prayer of letting go, and a prayer of letting God. Such prayer relinquishes control. In letting go, there would be an acknowledgment that parental figures cannot construct straight highways for their children's life journeys. Instead, children will quite often take muddy and messy detours. The growing up story for so many is through the messy stable—out on an uncharted road, and even exile in a foreign place—before they can ever come home again. Children are like pottery; their shaping begins at home, but they will be fired in other kilns.

PRAYER OF PARENTS—MESSY POTTERS

Avoid it if you can—
can't shapes the void we're in
order is the chaos we befriend. [11]

MARY RICHARDS [11]

The center point of our younger days
converged in the shaping of our children's lives.

We formed and molded them in our own image
caressing them with our most vibrant touch.

We were the potters—they were the clay
or so we thought in those early days.

Then they spun away out of our hands;
We do not have the finishing touch.

The clay has a dynamism all its own.
What it shall hold is not for us to say.

After the molding, they must be fired
in ovens not of our making or desire.

Sometimes, the pottery of their lives
is fractured, cast aside.

Awaiting the Lord's healing touch…
Jesus, mend the pieces together in Your design.

Father, pour the Holy Spirit into these precious vessels.
Fill them to the brim with new energy for better days.

WILLIAM JOHN FITZGERALD

THEY ARE NOT DEAD; THEY ARE ASLEEP

Sometimes our children seem to be dead, but they are only asleep for awhile. That is why parents keep praying for their children. This is beautifully illustrated in the gospel story of the raising of the daughter of Jairus. Even though he is ridiculed, Jairus seeks the Lord's intervention in the apparent death of his daughter.

"My daughter has just died; but come and lay your hand on her, and she will live."…When Jesus came to the leader's house and saw the flute players and the crowd making a commotion, he said, "Go away; for the girl is not dead but sleeping." And they laughed at him. (Mt 9:18, 23, 24)

Then, in his own time, and his own way, Jesus restores the daughter to health. It may sometimes appear that our children or grandchildren have been deadened to all of our hopes for their well-being. Yet Jesus may very well be quietly at work piecing scattered shards together in a design that will only be apparent later. Like the daughter of Jairus, he may say of our own loved ones: "They are only sleeping; they are not dead, no need to make such a din." There may be a day beyond our human reckoning when he says to them at age 20, 30, 40, or maybe even at the last hour, "Little boy, little girl, get up. Arise from sleep." On the day that the Jairus reading appears in the mass lectionary, the first reading accompanying it is the story of David and Absalom. Both stories are tales of parental hope in the midst of chaotic loss.

THE PHYSICAL DEATH OF THE YOUNG

Sometimes, in the hurry of youth, we actually lose young ones to tragic violent death, as David lost Absalom. No matter what the circumstances of their deaths, whether they were sober, or alert, gang victim, or accident victim, or bearer of some premature terminal illness, surely Jesus who cared for the daughter of Jairus is patient with their youth:

> *One night, Jesus who was young—could not wait*
> *for his disciples to arrive.*
> *He hurried forth from the tomb,*
> *And now he is out ahead*
> *of all the young*
> *who have hurried forth too soon.*
> *And he smiles and says to them:*
> *"Hurry home! Hurry home!"*[12]

If there are still any lingering regrets, any rifts, any need for healing with a departed loved one, Jesus has the power to heal them, for His Father's house is a mansion with many rooms. It is a blessed home of reconciliation, not a haunted house of alienation. He can bring home again those we cannot.

RECONCILIATION

Reconciliation, at the edge of alienation, whether with the living or the dead, is a peaceful homecoming. Will we ever be reconciled until we let go and let God? Sometimes our children dwell in stables or walk on alien roads. They may stumble and fall, and amazingly, some of those worst moments provide turning points in their lives. Parents are seldom in control of those moments when amazing grace intervenes. Grace is God's surprising gift in the midst of messiness. Sometimes, our children have to experience quite a bit of messiness and even chaos before they can ever discover grace. It is amazing grace because it breaks through at unexpected times and places.

ALIEN PLACES

In the gospels, Jesus and His saving grace were often found where least expected—such as in a stable in Bethlehem. Later, the infancy narratives situate Him as a youthful alien in Egypt. He would spend most of His young life in Nazareth. "Can anything good come out of Nazareth?" the apostle asked.

In His young adulthood, Jesus shocked the Pharisees when they found Him among messy tax collectors and prostitutes. He could also be found in hostile Samaria.

There is no place today too alien or far off where His presence cannot be found. No matter how far we wander into the wastelands, He can bring forth living waters in barren places. Our baptisms have left deep well-springs within us. Beneath the surface, faith has been planted very deep. Who knows where or when the Lord may draw up living waters from our hidden depths?

REFLECTION PAUSE

Pause for a moment. Who of your loved ones wander in alien places? Allow yourself five minutes of quiet time. Go into your imagination and imagine those loved ones journeying through a desert. Imagine them coming to an oasis. See Jesus drawing clear sparkling water from a well and offering it to them. Speak to Jesus about them. Tell Him why you love them and why they are so special.

Then tell the Lord, you must let go and put them in His hands, in His care. Place their hands in His. Step back. Admit to the Lord that you cannot plot their course. Ask Him in His time and in His way to show them the road that leads to a happy homecoming.

THE HEALING ROAD OF LETTING GO

To let go and to let be allows us to slip down from the pinnacle where we must be able to see the whole picture. In order for us to be understanding and forgiving we must pass over to where our children are and pass back again. John Donne writes of this when he says,

If a man were to pass over by sympathetic understanding into other lives and cultures and religions to the point where he could actually understand the interest in those interests, the attraction in these attractions, the sense in these ways, where he could find a resonance to them within himself, then he could truly say, "I find nothing human alien to me." [13]

We must pass over the alien ground where we sometimes find our children and realize that OUR God can be in an alien place, even though that may be apart from where we usually stand. Jesus Himself compared Himself to a mother hen concerned about her wandering chicks. Even His own disciples often stood apart on alien ground. They were going their own way most of the time. Between Ascension and Pentecost the disciples dwelt in a house of alienation, cut off, not knowing the Father's will. Sometimes, children do the same. So do parents.

PENTECOST FOR FAMILIES

So many parents need to be delivered from false guilt as they see their own chicks stray. Even if parents have done their very best, their children are immersed in a culture with its own siren songs. Other parents may have genuine guilt about alcoholic or sexual abuse on their own part and the dysfunction it brought into their children's lives. There are twelve steps beyond this kind of chaos, and there is sacramental absolution and reconciliation. Such guilt ridden parents must also go through the ultimate letting go of forgiving themselves. Christ came, not for the self-righteous, but to save and to heal sinners.

No matter what the past held for parents or children, there can come a day when the winds blow, the house shakes and all generations hear and understand each other, even though speaking in different languages. A pathway can emerge. The house of alienation can open into a home of reconciliation. Parents and children can pass through messy stables and come home again. That may not be until the end of time. It may be sooner.

PRAYER FOR PASSING OVER

O God, Our Caring Parent:
Let us pass over to where our children are.
Let us pass over to where other religions are.
Let us pass over to where other cultures are.
Let us pass over to all different people in alien places.

Let us pass over the worries that keep us from golden ponds of aging
   contentment.
Let us pass over the "what ifs" that wither the autumn foliage of our
   later years.
Let us pass over the heritage gap on the healing road of "letting go" and
   "letting be."
Let us pass through the troubled waters of ambiguity—
through paradox, toward peace.

Let us "seize the moment" for reconciliation and healing.

Let us let go of our stern inner parent,
that voice within decreeing: "Guilty!" "Guilty!" "Guilty!" for what we
have done, and what we have failed to do.
Let us let go of needing our children to exceed our goals. Let us let go of
the clay on the potter's wheel.
We have spun enough.

WILLIAM JOHN FITZGERALD

PERSONAL REFLECTION—FOR FAMILY MEMBERS

What area in my children's, grandchildren's, or family member's life do I most need to cross over and be gentle toward?

What would most help to bring reconciliation into my life at this time?

What do I need to do to put false guilt behind me?

SCRIPTURE REFLECTIONS

Lk 15:11–32	PARABLE OF PRODIGAL SON
2 Sm 18:33;19:1	DAVID AND ABSALOM
Jn 20:19–23	RECONCILIATION
Jn 9:1–41	MAN—BLIND FROM BIRTH

4

The Way Home—
Letting Go and Forgiving

The way that leads us home to finding spirituality is a path of forgiveness and letting go. We need forgiveness to thaw the ice that blocks the way to this path. Unless we learn to forgive, we will slip and slide like an awkward child. In fact, it is hard to grow up unless we learn to forgive.

On this journey home most of us also have some messy childhood tapes which may need re-editing or even changing so that we can be fully at home with ourselves.

SONYA

Sonya is an only child. She and her parents live in the Twin Cities in Minnesota where the winters are long, the days short, and the ice covers 10,000 lakes. Before she even entered school, Sonya learned to skate. At age four, she would hold onto her parents' hands and slide along the ice on tiny blades. Her little muffler would wave in the wind, a tiny flag announcing, "I'm here and I'm moving!" Her tiny cheeks peeked out over the muffler like two shiny apples. Indeed, she was, and still is, the apple of her parents' eyes. Between the ages of five and thirteen, Sonya grew in wisdom in the classroom and in skill and grace on the ice rink. At thirteen, her blond hair would twirl about and cascade around her neck as she would spin and glide along the ice. She was a natural, and day by day, she was getting better and better.

By her thirteenth winter, she loved skating so much that she would often come home late from school, having spent the after school time on the ice rink that was part of her junior high campus. On a very frigid January day, before Sonya left for school, her mother reminded her, "Remember Sonya, today is the day your Dad gets home early from work. We'll pick you up at school exactly at 4:00 PM because we have to go to the mall and get some shopping done, and then we are going to go to the Winter Carnival in Saint Paul."

Four o'clock came and Sonya's parents arrived at the school entrance right on time. No Sonya. Her mother, a little exasperated, and somewhat worried, asked a student standing at the door, "Do you know where our daughter Sonya is?" "Oh sure. She is out behind the school on the ice rink."

The parents drove around to the back of the school, and sure enough, there was Sonya in the center of a crowd of kids. She was doing some spins on the ice that not even her parents had seen before. Also, there was a beautiful young woman clad in a red and blue jacket. She had her skates on, and was watching and admiring Sonya's graceful exhibition.

When her father arrived at the edge of the rink, he was polite but stern, "Sonya, your mother and I have been searching all around for you!" Sonya replied, "But dad, didn't you remember that I practice my skating for a little while every night after school?" "Not tonight, Sonya; tonight you are to go shopping with your mother and I." There was a pause. Then Sonya excused herself, went to the sideboard of the rink, took off her skates, tied their laces together and tossed the unscuffed white leather shoes over her shoulder. She then turned to the beautiful young woman who had been watching her skating with such intense interest, and said, "Sorry, I have to leave. I have to go shopping with my folks." The young woman smiled. "I understand, but I sure would have liked to observe your skating a little longer. I was very impressed by your skill. You are a young skater with a lot of promise." Sonya said, "Thanks, coming from you, that means a lot." And then Sonya and her parents drove away in their car.

The young woman ice skater was a member of the U.S. Olympic team making a once in a lifetime visit to this junior high school. (And this story is a parable.)

───────────── ✺ ─────────────

REFLECTION PAUSE

Did Sonya's parents know the young olympian's identity? Did they find out later? How did Sonya feel about losing this opportunity to continue performing for such an important guest? This is a parable, and you will have to supply your own answers. How would you have felt if you were Sonya?

What happened later? Did Sonya continue to develop her skating skills, or did she miss her golden opportunity to be recognized? And if she did, was it her parents' fault? Were they guilty of a great injustice to her? Is there a Sonya story in your experience?

───────────── ✐ ─────────────

ANOTHER CHILD

Once upon a time, another child, a thirteen-year-old boy entered into the circle of a distinguished group of elders. The boy had brown inquisitive eyes deep set in a dark face. His lush hair fell down toward his shoulders. He would very much resemble a young Jewish boy you might see on the streets of New York returning from his Bar Mitzvah, smiling, with his yarmulke jauntily perched on his head. He wore no head dress, however, and this meeting would prove to be a premature and short-lived rite of passage. Just the whisper of a fuzz was beginning to show on his bronzed face. His hands were leathery for a lad his age. If one looked closely, a tiny wound on his hand was healing from a sliver. Healing would not take long, for he was healthy and vigorous, his muscles finely honed from lifting and some sort of manual labor. As he asked questions of the circle of men, and as they, with more and more interest, began to quiz him, they marveled at the wisdom and grace he showed for such a tender age.

When he did not return to either his father or mother, they questioned each other, "I thought he was with your family members." "And I thought he was with yours!" They looked at each other bewildered. This had never happened before. His mother, who was only in her late twenties, furrowed her brow. This entirely new experience was confusing. She was not prepared for it. This was her only son, and now he seemed to be lost. She was seized with a moment of panic. "Come!" she said to her husband, "We've got to find him!"

After searching for a long time through streets and public buildings, they came around a corner and there he was sitting surrounded by a group of grownups—all older men. Again, his mother's heart skipped a beat. Who were these men? It was not safe for any lad to take up with strangers. She had heard tales of abductions and even worse. As they approached closer, she recognized some of the men. Her fears eased. Some of them were quite prominent citizens. Still, it did not seem proper for her child, a carpenter's son, to be sitting in such a high place. Their society had a rigid set of values based on honor and shame. What if her young son had blundered into this group? What if he were shamed by such an experience? Being a good Jewish mother, she wanted only what was best for her son.

She looked at him with love and said, "Your dad and I have been searching for you. It is time to come home with us now." Her son paused, and then he said a very strange thing, "Didn't you know I must be about my father's business?" They didn't. They only knew that he belonged at home with them within the security of their house.

There was a long pause. Teenagers sometimes say such strange things. His mother pondered these words for a few moments, and then said, "Please come home with us now." Her son got up, smiled a farewell glance at the distinguished citizens surrounding him, and followed his mom and dad up a narrow street.

How did he feel as he walked up that street? What did he think? Were his feelings similar to Sonya's? We don't know. We can only guess. We know he was fully human and his feelings ran the gamut of what other Jewish boys his age might feel in that time and that place.

Was this a missed opportunity? Might one of these learned gentlemen have taken him under his wing and tutored him? Would he have penetrated the corridors of power and been in a position later to yield persuasive leverage? Would he have wanted to be a power within the establishment? In all of our lives, we never know about the road not taken, do we?

What we do know is that when he walked up that narrow street, he was not to be heard from again for seventeen years. And we do know that when he did emerge, it was evident by who he was and by what he said that his life at home with those parents had proved to be a great blessing. He knew the traditions of his people and was familiar with the scriptures. He was ready and well prepared to leave home on a heroic quest.

MESSY PARENTING

In both of these situations these were parents who cared about their children. There was also no way that they could be aware of all of the circumstances of the situations. Only God knows all the nuances of our human stories. These were good parents doing the best they could for their children according to the knowledge that was avail-

able to them at the time. If you were to put parenting on a continuum, it might look something like this:

NORMAL MESSINESS   CHAOS

GOOD PARENTS INVOLVED   ABUSIVE
IN THE DAY-BY-DAY   PARENTS
CHALLENGE OF MESSY PARENTING

Even the best of parents—like Mary and Joseph are not capable
of seeing the whole picture. Some degree of messiness is a given for
all good parents. At the other end of the continuum are abusive parents who actually, in some sense, curse their children. Recalling the
mother on the train, did she bear some responsibility for her son's
death? Probably not. But if she did, forgiveness of self is the only
possible release from an inner self-inflicted punishment that is like
capital punishment for the soul.

Parenting seems to be a learn-as-you-go process. Young parents
are equipped with stamina and endurance. Wisdom accrues from
experience. Between stamina and wisdom there is a lot of messiness.

CHAOS

Most parents try to bless their children. Some parents, because of the
twistedness in their own lives, curse their children. Adolph Hitler
was beaten and abused by a drunken father. Severe dysfunction pro-
duces unrelenting chaos. A helpline for the abused advises:

Childhood abuse…is so emotionally jarring that the effects can last a lifetime. If you were sexually abused…you likely have a poor image of yourself, even today. You may become depressed too often, or have a hard time
sustaining meaningful relationships. Sometimes you turn to drugs and
alcohol to mask the pain. [14]

PARENT TAPES

Even when good parents try to do their very best, they can pass on to their children good "tapes" that are a little skewed or distorted by their own previous experience. My own mother was a devoted parent and I am grateful for the blessings she bestowed on me. Whenever we would travel she had several prayers we would say together as we got in the car. However, those prayers carried with them a coloring of fear. My mother had a great fear of accidents. As a child it seemed excessive to me, and I could not understand it, but some of that fear also became imprinted on my own interior tapes.

It was only in later life that I was able to piece together the origins of my mother's fears. As a child, she had seen her uncle go off to work one day. At day's end all that returned was the news of him being suddenly killed, crushed between two box-cars. She had also seen her own father, a railroad worker, have his hand mangled— eventually requiring amputation of his arm. She had seen her active mother come down with a serious crippling disease, and her father die suddenly without warning.

Despite such fearful life wounds, she was courageous in giving birth to a baby while in frail health due to life threatening blood clots. And she did so in 1932—during the depths of the Depression. (Sometimes it is necessary to venture into the dark cave of fear in order to discover the true grit of courage.)

Part of my own growing up process later in life has been to come to understand her fears and to sort out my own interior tapes which still bore some of her fears. My mother almost drowned as a child. I was forty years old before I put away my old fear tapes and learned to swim. The time does come when we ought to put away fearful childhood tapes.

When I was a child, I spoke like a child, I thought like a child, I reasoned like a child; when I became an adult, I put an end to childish ways. (1 Cor 13:11)

SLURRED TAPES

Sometimes tapes from childhood are slurred. As children, we played a game called Kick-the-Can. We had a chant that went with the game. We yelled, "Ollie, ollie, oxen free!" because that is what the older kids taught us, and they chanted it because that is what the older kids taught them. Only a few years ago did I learn that this game has been passed down from ancient times from generation to generation. Over the years, the "Ollie, ollie oxen free" tape had become slurred. In its original colonial times form, the words were, "All Ye, All Ye Outs in free!"

We may all have some slurred parental tapes that need to be edited. Some are quite good and need only some adjustment. Some others may even need to be thrown out.

REFLECTION PAUSE

Letting Go! From time to time, you sort out your closets and get rid of old garments. Sometimes its hard to let go because they have sentimental value, but you may realize they really are no longer usable, and so you let them go. Have you ever thought about sorting out old messages encoded in your brain?

Can you think of any old sayings you learned in childhood? Do all of them still apply?

How about, "I am not good enough." "It is my fault." "Our family secret is..." "You should be ashamed." Can any of these tapes be changed to a positive affirmation?

Bring Jesus into your prayer and allow Him to tell you over and over an affirming message that contradicts your flawed tape. You well might make this a daily prayer experience.

Perhaps the most demanding of parental tapes is "Be perfect." Do you expect this of yourself? Do you expect it of others? Have the authority figures in your life expected it of you? Bring Jesus again into your prayer, and let Him tell you, "I love you as you are—regardless of your flaws and imperfections!"

YOU CAN'T BE PERFECT!

"Be perfect!" is a common parental message most of us receive over a lifetime from many authority figures. We are also exposed to a constant drumbeat of commercials. We are told, "You can even buy perfection." The products displayed by beautiful people will show you how, but this is an illusion.

In our work lives people are expected to do more and more—with greater demands for perfection. Since no one is a perfect worker, we lag and fall short of unrealistic demands.

BUMPS

I shared pre-marriage instructions with a very bright young couple. He was an airline pilot. She was an air traffic controller. She mentioned, "You know, it ruins his day if he has the slightest bump on landing." We talked about that. I agreed with him, that every passenger would love to fly with a pilot that never bumps, but that one bump would not ruin their day, nor should it his.

Old messages about being perfect make it difficult to forgive our own imperfect bumps. Impatience about our inadequacies can easily lead to anger over others not being on a perfect path. Notice how many angry and grim drivers there are on the freeways.

REFLECTION PAUSE

You might examine your own patience quotient. As a confessor for almost four decades, the most common fault that I have heard confessed over and over is, "I am so very impatient." Anger often follows. In the Sacrament of Reconciliation, we receive forgiveness, but do we really forgive ourselves?

Perhaps we all need to be more forgiving with our own bumps, messiness, and imperfections. The Navajos always make one bad stitch in their wonderful blankets, "for only God can make a perfect blanket."

PRAYER FOR PATIENCE

The tower of Pisa leans.
The Liberty Bell is cracked.
Mona Lisa sneaks a smile.
Yet pilgrims gaze and admire.

Abe Lincoln was disheveled.
Harry Truman failed haberdashery,
and FDR could not walk.
Yet their glory is enshrined.

When I sew a bad stitch in my life blanket,
or bump against my imperfections—
instead of replaying old tyrannical tapes,
help me switch from "Replay" to "Delete."

Help me to cope with messiness,
(mine and everyone else's)
and know the difference between
genuine chaos—and just a bad bounce.

WILLIAM JOHN FITZGERALD

SEEING THINGS DIFFERENTLY

As we continue our life journeys, we need to see things differently, rather than continually replay old childhood parental tapes. I used to take a twenty minute walk around the perimeter of a desert retreat house. I always walked in a counter-clockwise direction. One day, I decided to walk in a clockwise direction. I was amazed that I saw different aspects of the same scene on my new way of walking. I now saw the sunny sides of the cactus instead of the shadows. The same rabbits ran in a different direction. Carl Hammerschlag, a psychiatrist, in his book, *The Theft of the Spirit,* tells us that if you really want to know something, look at it again. We spend so much time learning things one way that we automatically spend the rest of our energy getting others to see things *"our way"*—and as the only possible way.

There is an amazing phenomenon about growing up to be parents. In our teen years we are often in rebellion about our parents' outmoded ideas, and then a funny thing happens on our way through parenthood. Quite often, new parents will repeat again the mode of parenting that they experienced from their own parents. While a lot of that is good, some of it is in need of rewrite.

GRUMPY OLD MEN

At a reconciliation service I asked the people to reflect on grumpiness which gets in the way of forgiveness, and called their attention to the comedy, *Grumpy Old Men,* set in the wintertime in Minnesota.

Walter Matthau and Jack Lemmon had been friends from childhood, but now in their elder years are turning into grumpy old men. Walter Matthau harbors old memories from childhood and from their courtship days, and he has never forgiven Jack Lemmon for ancient slights—at least the way he saw it. They spend a lot of their time fishing out on the ice and Walter's ancient grudges and present jealousy erupt in a scene in which he tries to push Jack Lemmon and his ice fishing cabin right into the melting lake.

Harboring old grudges and unforgiving memories is a lot like ice fishing at its worst. We sit and sit, and gripe and grump, and all we bring up from the depths are sour memories that smell like rancid carp. Bad family memories are like rotting fish. Sometimes they are of parental mistakes; sometimes they go all the way back to sibling rivalries. We need to let go of them, throw them back in the lake and not keep bringing them home over and over.

OTHER PARENTAL FIGURES

As Catholics, we may also have other encoded messages from parental figures in Mother Church: from father, sister, or brother. Most of them are very good, some are slurred, some might be abusive. The same continuum can be applied to these parental figures:

NORMAL MESSINESS   CHAOS

GOOD DEDICATED CLERGY   ABUSIVE
INVOLVED IN THE DAILY   CLERGY
CHALLENGE OF MESSY
TEACHING AND MODELING

Some Catholics have old horror tapes of life with Sister. Some were cracked on the knuckles at school and at home too. Perhaps the old memories of Sister's ruler stand out because we knew our parents were not perfect, but we expected Sister to be. And then the old sisters are gone, and we never get to hear their side of the story.

Last week I heard a 55-year-old man recalling his high school years, "We were terrors," he said. "We had a young sister right out of the novitiate and we boys harassed her. When she prepared a process for electing a May Crowning queen, we conspired and elected an ugly football player as our queen. We sometimes made her days long, but deep down, we knew she liked us, and although we would never admit it, we liked her too. A few months ago, our class celebrated our thirtieth reunion by taking a cruise together. We wanted her and one of the other sisters with us. We wanted to pay their way, but they couldn't come—still keeping their poverty vow. I still treasure her good influence on my formative years and count her as a friend."

I too had the sisters in grade school and it is a wonder to me that they did the good work that they did. They slept in a dormitory style attic with no air-conditioning, worked for $50.00 per month, and were thrown into classrooms with the minimum of preparation. The wonder is not that a few knuckles were cracked, but that they accomplished so very much teaching despite so many obstacles.

ABUSE

Just as with parents, there have always been lots of clergy doing their work with some messiness as a given. And there have been some who became models of parental care. Father Flanagan took on a parental role and established perhaps the most famous home in America—Father Flanagan's Home for Boys—better known as Boys Town. His life work symbolizes the good parental influence assumed by many priests, brothers, and nuns in many orphanages and schools.

Despite the wonderful influence of the Father Flanagans, there have also been a minority of abusers. Just as in families, in our church, messiness was denied and chaos was doubly denied as nonexistent. The deeply tragic pedophilia revelations of recent years have shattered that denial. These revelations go way beyond messiness. They reveal the utter depths of chaos and havoc in the lives of the abused. I once visited with a gentleman who told me he had stayed away from church for forty years because of advances made to him in college by a priest—a long time to be away from home. But he went on to say he had come home again, and was happy to be back gathered around the altar. All of us clergy need to ask forgiveness for our own messiness, and forgiveness for the incalculable damage done by abusers.

HEALING, RECOVERY, FORGIVENESS

When children have experienced sexual abuse, physical abuse, emotional abuse, when they have been enmeshed in dysfunctional situations, they are severely wounded beyond the bumps and bruises of normal messy living. Therapy, recovery, and renewal are demanded. The children of alcoholics have a strong tendency to become alcoholic themselves. The abused tend to abuse. It is the tape they know. For so many of us, it takes twelve steps, and many years—one day at a time—before we can author our own better stories. Whether it is at the beginning of the healing process or during it, or every day of our lives, there is need for a further spiritual dimension. To cope with our messiness and to move from chaos, forgiveness is the creative spiritual seed we can all plant in our muddy human soil.

We need to forgive our parents and parental figures for their messiness, and even in some instances for their chaos. How many times? Seventy times seven. And it may take even more forgiveness than that until we get it right.

We need to sift through our old parental tapes and eventually become our OWN parents. We shall speak with authority and authenticity in our lives only when we ultimately author our own stories. If old parental messages or actions continue to fuel anger, disappointment, bitterness in our current lives, then we are still children tossed to and fro by old memories. Our inner parental messages echo like the ravings of tyrants and our inner child continues to bleed and suffer. Forgiveness, letting go, letting God be the final judge is ultimately a freeing process. We can come home again through forgiveness.

ON GOLDEN POND–FORGIVENESS

There is a story behind the movie plot of *On Golden Pond* I have shared at several reconciliation services with my parishioners. The making of this movie brought Jane Fonda and her father Henry together for one last time shortly before his death, and provided a golden opportunity for reconciliation.

As a result of the movie, Jane Fonda also came home to an acceptance of the ambiguity of her relationship with her father. For Jane, the real-life drama between her and her dad far exceeded the movie plot. Early in her childhood, she had lost her mother to a tragic suicide. Her father, being an actor, was often absent during her growing-up years. Communication had not been strong in the Fonda family. The making of the movie, *On Golden Pond* provided a unique opportunity for father and daughter to share, both a cinematic and a real-life reunion. However, it was to fall short of Jane's hopes and expectations.

A key scene in the movie had Chelsea, played by Jane, wading out into the water to meet her father, and appealing, "Why can't we just be friends?" Because of her real flesh and blood relationship to her father, she found this a very difficult scene to play. She had to summon up all her acting and emotional energy just to get through this scene. Once she had done it, she sensed a deep feeling of relief and reunion. She had passed through a moment of emotional chaos that seemed to open into feelings of relief and joyful reunion. It seemed to be a moment of reconciliation and coming home. At the end of the day, after the movie shooting was completed, she could not wait to share this experience with her father. Over dinner, she did so, and then asked Henry Fonda if he had ever felt or experienced what she had felt that day. His only response: "Nope."

Jane described her reaction to his curt response in an article in *TV Guide*. She wrote about how, at moments like this, she felt out on a limb, all by herself. There was a gulf and she would try to relieve the pain by reminding herself that her dad just did not know how to reach out. However she learned something very valuable from these impasses with her dad:

One thing I've learned though, and fortunately I learned it before he died, is that blame and judgment are no way to go through life. Forgiveness is important. You can't grow up until you forgive. [15]

She went on to say that once you yourself become a parent you discover you are not perfect either; you have your own journey to make, your own ghosts to exorcise. Jane Fonda is a person some have grown to respect and love; for others, she remains a person they love to hate. Images of a youthful Jane visiting the enemy during the Vietnam War are indelibly stamped upon many people's memories. In some ways, Jane symbolizes the gulf that sometimes widens between the generations.

For those who cannot forgive her, or more importantly can't forgive their own parents, their children, or themselves, her observation is appropriate, *"You can't grow up until you forgive."*

PRAYER REFLECTION—YOU CAN'T GROW UP UNTIL YOU FORGIVE

Our family: (names) ....
like old rosary beads,
worn out from rough handling,
no longer a circle,
links broken,
once together,
then a prayer,
now a jumble.

Sometimes, the mysteries of our family
were glorious, sometimes joyful,
now the cadence is of sorrow,
Our Lady, sword pierced,
Mother of Sorrows,
bind our wounds.
I pray for: ....
Lead us home.

PERSONAL REFLECTION—WHERE AM I ON THE ICE?

tripping a lot because of the dull skates given to me by my parents.

ice-fishing down deep into the depths of the past, and pulling out smelly carp.

with Walter Matthau out on the cold ice, but hot with anger inside when I think of past family slights. I wish I could push..........in the lake!

skating through life, sometimes falling, but getting up again, and not blaming anyone in the past for my own present pratfalls.

skating along, remembering that when mom and dad taught me to skate, they were not olympians; they taught me as best they could. It's now up to me to improve on their efforts.

doing figure eights and triple axles a lot of the time and sometimes racking up a 9.5 score—skating free with the wind, (tripping now and then and getting a 5.0 score), but whatever I get, it's MY score!

After figuring out where you are, where would you like to be with icy memories—and how might you get there?

Scripture Reflections

Mk 11:25	PRAYER AND FORGIVENESS
Lk 11:1–4	OUR FATHER
Jas 2:8–13	MERCY
Jn 9:1–34	MAN BORN BLIND

5

Mess Hall—
Coming Home from Hunger

One day Mary came to see her pastor. She had been at daily mass and yet never went to holy communion. She explained why. Both she and her husband were previously married in their youth and subsequently divorced. Mary and Tom have since been in a civil marriage for twenty-four years. She told him she approached a priest some years ago and she got the mistaken impression that nothing could be done not only for her, but also for Tom who also needed an annulment. Quite to the contrary, something could be done. A year later two annulments came through, and Mary and Tom celebrated the sacrament of matrimony. They were happier than any couple I've ever seen on their twenty-fifth anniversary.

THE HERO'S OR HEROINE'S QUEST
We leave our parental homes to engage life, to challenge its limits, to seek its rewards. This is the hero's or heroine's quest, a myth threaded through most human stories. This outward journey is sometimes messy and usually bruising. In our striving for careers, for success, and for marriage and family fulfillment, we can be

wounded. And sooner or later we may grow faint and hungry. There comes a time when we yearn to come home again, to heal our wounds, and to be welcomed at a friendly and nourishing table.

A wonderful image of the hero's or heroine's quest is found in the story of King Arthur, the Knights of the Round Table and their quest for the Holy Grail. After all their adventures, they too come home again bearing wounds. For Lancelot, his secret love for Guinevere is a wound of the heart. In a poignant exchange between King Arthur and Sir Lancelot, the knight begs leave of the round table:

"My Lord, King," he said, "Forgive me if I ask leave to go. An old wound has broken open." Arthur smiled down on him. "I have the same old wound," he said. "We'll go together." [16]

Sir Lancelot, the noblest knight of the realm, after making heroic quests, alas was also wounded, for he had betrayed the king through his secret love for the king's wife Queen Guinevere. However, Arthur chooses to walk with him as his wounded companion. Like Lancelot, all of us, at some time or other have the need to come home again to a friendly table. The need is all the greater because a friendly table can be a holy place of healing.

BABETTE'S FEAST

There is a classic movie called *Babette's Feast* that is sometimes used in religion classes on the Eucharist.

In the movie, an outsider, an exile from France, prepares a wonderful meal for the quarreling neighbors in a Danish village. They enjoy the meal and gradually begin to savor each other's presence. Moved by a toast, the participants begin to forgive old grudges and even join in laughter. As they prepare to take their leave, they join hands and sing an old hymn, "Let us use our time so that our true home we may find."

OUR EUCHARISTIC TABLE

We too are finally and fully at our true home when we gather around our table with those we love. However, some Catholics experience deep alienation wounds resulting from what they perceive as either unworthiness, or legal obstacles that keep them from gathering at their own eucharistic table. Some divorced Catholics suffer from alienation because they believe that divorce or remarriage for a Catholic automatically incurs excommunication. It does not.

Recently I welcomed back to holy communion a woman who was divorced years ago, whose husband subsequently had died. Yet this single widow attended mass for the last eighteen years—never going to holy communion—thinking she could not! When I asked her why she had not sought counsel, she replied, "Even though I yearned for holy communion, the rules seemed too intimidating."

Some shrink from pursuing annulments because they believe such a decree would declare their children to be illegitimate. This is not so. Others in some second marriages grieve because they may judge themselves to be ineligible to receive the eucharist. There are others who have the misperception that only the affluent can afford the costs of an annulment. (In fact, there are costs for the administrative procedures, but these are adjusted for the poor, and no one need shrink from seeking an annulment for lack of ability to pay.)

NO LONGER AT HOME
There are too many Catholics who no longer feel at home in the Catholic community because of their experience of failed marriages. Their number is growing. According to research reported by Gallup and Castelli, in the last decade, one adult Catholic in ten was divorced, separated, and single. The number has grown since then.

According to a landmark study in the last decade by Dean Hoge: *Converts, Dropouts, Returnees,* many divorcees were among the three major groups of people dropping out of active Catholic life. Hoge found many of these felt little support from their Catholic community and at the time of their divorce suffered from intense feelings of alienation and loneliness.

In the opinion of the pollster George Gallup, Americans in general are the loneliest people in the world! Gallup's surveys have found that Americans have a deep desire for a sense of community from their church affiliation. They consequently turn to their churches for fellowship. Perhaps that is why the American bishops in their pastoral letter *Go and Make Disciples* indicate they want greater hospitality at the Sunday eucharist and at all liturgical celebrations.

The perception of an isolated and messy status in the church raises pertinent pastoral questions. Must the alienated among the divorced leave us and seek solace elsewhere? And what of devout remarried Catholics who are in stable unions and are regularly at mass? Is there any way they can find their place at the eucharistic table? Do you have friends and relatives who, like Tom and Mary, go to church, but do not receive the holy eucharist, or who don't go to church, or who have joined fundamentalist churches because they feel they cannot go to holy communion in the Catholic Church?

REFLECTION PAUSE

Pause for a few minutes; bring them to mind . . . speak to the Lord about them.

SANCTUARY

This chapter is about God writing straight on crooked lines, and about the good shepherd who seeks out the alienated and separated ones and feeds them. Is there a light and a sanctuary in our church for some who feel they are outside in the dark? There is an ancient tradition of our church buildings being sanctuaries for people in trouble. Some years ago, even the accused drug dealer Manuel Noriega, pursued by American troops, sought and obtained sanctuary in the Vatican Embassy in Panama. An uproar ensued. How could the church give sanctuary to Noriega?

And yet isn't the church's door supposed to be open to sinners? A church sanctuary is not only a holy place, it is also a refuge for sinners. Noriega must have sensed that when he encountered what Shakespeare called the "image of hell," and "the comfort killing night." Surely those you know and love who seem to be estranged from Holy Communion are not to be imprisoned like Noriega. They are like you and me, wounded pilgrims on a life journey.

Can we hope that the Christ light will see them and us through our worst night? Is there not a little of the alienating night shadow that lurks close to all of us? Is the role of the church to consign us to that blurry existence, or rather to help us to find a passage through? It is a beautiful Catholic tradition that our churches are usually unlocked, our tabernacle lights burning before a real presence, our sanctuaries open to all who seek solace in the midst of their messiness or chaos. These holy places are sanctuaries where we can steady ourselves from hell's pursuit. Our church's doors are open when all other doors are slammed shut. They are meant to be sanctuaries of spiritual nourishment as well as open doors that lead to compassionate pastoral care. The road to that door is messy. So are all who enter. Webster's Dictionary defines a mess hall as "a place where a group eats regularly." Perhaps our churches should be called mess halls rather than basilicas or cathedrals.

A POPE'S WITNESS TO MERCY
Pope John Paul II asked for a more merciful, compassionate, and pastoral church in his encyclical *Rich in Mercy*. Beyond words about mercy he witnessed to compassionate pastoral care in an even more dramatic way when he paid a pastoral visit to the man who attempted to assassinate him. To this attempted murderer he offered acceptance and forgiveness.

THE MESSY EMMAUS ROAD
After his resurrection, the first meal of Jesus was in a mess hall, an inn that made room for broken disciples needing pastoral care. He brought them in from their highway journey where they had been walking with their heads down, seeing only the camel dung on the road, their minds filled with the horrible memories of the Friday crucifixion. It was only when this "stranger" joined them on the road and began to search the scriptures for the meaning to the alienating events of Good Friday, that their hearts began to burn. In their

conversation, he began to make a connection between their inner pain and the meaning of the cross.

As they would recall later, it was only at the table that they recognized him in the breaking of the bread. He, in turn, recognized them in the breaking of their hearts. It was precisely in their brokenness that they were fed. To be broken is to not yet have it all together. Ever since then, many in need of pastoral care have come to eucharist with their own brokenness to be nourished and healed by the breaking of the holy bread.

REFLECTION PAUSE

> *While Jesus was eating, tax collectors and sinners sat with him [Mt 9:10-11] and the Pharisees complained about him eating with estranged people but Jesus offered them compassionate pastoral care.*
>
> *Pause and reflect on the Noriega and Emmaus stories.*
>
> *Who do you know going through their darkest night? Who do you know walking with their heads down on the road in need of compassionate pastoral care? (Note: the word "pastor" refers to a shepherd and the care he has for his sheep.) You might ask the Lord to lead them to a healing pastor who could offer pastoral care.*
>
> *Your friends or relatives are not scoundrels like Noriega. But sometimes, some of them feel as though they are perceived that way by their faith community. Imagine them going in to eat with Christ and recognizing Him in the breaking of the bread. Speak to the Lord about these friends of yours.*

SACRAMENT OF RECONCILIATION OR ALIENATION?

At a gathering of priests a pastor and liturgical scholar whose parish was near the Strategic Air Command headquarters spoke of the eucharist as a healing and reconciling sacrament. After his talk, one questioner remarked, "I'm aware that some of the S.A.C. generals go to daily communion even though they are involved in targeting entire cities for nuclear destruction. I would believe they have convinced themselves that they are keeping the peace and have moral reasons to do so, yet planning destruction of whole cities is at least questionable. But what of others who are in questionable situations? Should the generals receive healing from the eucharist and others whose life experiences do not possess the gravity of decisions about life and death be denied? Should we be more pastorally sensitive with the generals than with anyone else? Perhaps we also need church tribunals for the fifth commandment as well as for the sixth." The presenter's brow furrowed. There was no response.

MARRIAGE TRIBUNALS
Tribunals exist to safeguard the bond of matrimony, but also to help aggrieved parties secure rights within their church and to allow the law to be healing medicine. Too many Catholics fail to seek annulments because they have become alienated from the very institution that might bring them deep inner peace. According to a study contained in *U.S. Catholic Magazine* in the last decade, out of 8 million divorced Catholics, more than 6 million entered into second marriages. Fewer than 10 percent of those divorced Catholics have approached a marriage tribunal. For some dealing with a tribunal seems too threatening. And yet, marriage tribunals are often staffed with pastoral persons who are concerned both about the institution of marriage and the individual person. For so many people who have used them, the marriage tribunals have been fountains of life-giving water. The annulment process for many has been a source of deep personal healing. Many have come home again to peace with themselves and with their church. According to Joseph Zwack who did research on annulments for his book, *Annulment*, (Harper and Row, 1983) many of the marriage tribunals he studied, rendered favorable judgments to the petitioners in almost 95 percent of the cases they considered.

Because of the minimum efforts on the part of Catholics to seek annulments, there are prayers at the end of this chapter for those who may be unnecessarily hesitating to apply. The statistics above indicate that there may be many out there in the wilderness who could come home again to the eucharist, if they only knew the way out of the ruins of failed dreams.

Bishop Walter Kasper, as a younger theologian, wrote of the need for some kind of survival accommodation for some people trying to find life beyond the bitter ashes of a failed marriage. This image would seem to be in accord with the way God acts in the history of human salvation. As noted before, He often writes straight on crooked lines.

PRAYER REFLECTION—FROM THE ASHES

Marriage—young builders
set the foundations
for better, for worse,
cornerstoned in Christ.

Sometimes a tragic flaw,
the mortar is mortal;
it fails; it falls
down into rubble.

We were apprentices,
not master builders
we regret and relent
in sackcloth of failure.

Help us fill the breach,
rise from the ashes,
follow the Lord
from death to life.

Is there a house of bread,
a refuge, a sanctuary?
For we are very hungry.
Help us, Lord, to be fed.

THE AGONY OF DIVORCE
In some ways, divorce is to many families in our time what the Black Death was to the fourteenth century—destabilizing, pain inducing, and deeply alienating. Like an epidemic, it spreads. The U.S divorce rate is the highest in the world!

Some 1.2 million divorces were granted in 1994, according to the National Center for Health Statistics. That translates to virtually one of every two marriages, a rate more than twice that of other industrial countries. [17]

When a partner is cast off by a frivolous divorce, he or she is treated like a consumer item, something to be used (sometimes abused), and then thrown away when the chemistry of being in love fades and other allurements beckon beyond the marriage bond.

The children can become throwaways too—pawns to be shuffled back and forth between the jagged edges of separation. Father Val Peter who directs a "mash unit" for hurting kids at Boys Town can testify to this. His Boys Town call-in hotline for disturbed children (800–448–3000) has recorded over two million calls! Father Peter observes, "I see some adults being 'happy' and 'fulfilled' in some multiple marriages while their kids are so damaged that they attempt suicide, do drugs, get into alcohol and become sexually active because it deadens their pain. This happens because some parents were never challenged to grow up spiritually." This is not new. 2,000 years ago, Jesus observed husbands summarily dismissing their wives for flimsy reasons and His condemnation of such activity echoes down through the ages. So does His compassion for the wounded and the abused.

Children are wounded and bruised by divorce. They are often confused when a divorced parent accompanies them to mass and does not receive the eucharist. Alienation caused by divorce can be passed down through the generations.

BITTER ASHES

In contrast to some divorced people who have entered multiple marriages for selfish reasons, there are countless others who sought separation from their spouse as a last and necessary resort to maintain their own or their children's safety, security, health, or moral well-being. Some divorces spare children from abuse, yet quite often, the children falsely blame themselves for their parents' marriage failures. This imposes a double wound.

The wounded may also include partners who bear greater responsibility for their marriage failure because of earlier immaturity, or even those who at a later date recognize a previous marriage culpability and repent of it. These factors raise challenges for pastoral care. One of the pastoral considerations is whether remarriage after divorce, especially by an aggrieved party, must mean terminal alienation from the eucharistic table. The pastoral problem is aggravated when the religious training of children is involved. The numbers of wounded people are increasing. More and more people form a long alienation procession trudging through the dusty valleys of marriage disappointment and failure. If they do not find their way home to the eucharist, in some locations only a minority of the faith community may be receiving holy communion. That would not seem to correspond with the way that Jesus shared the eucharist. On Holy Thursday, He gathered a group of walking wounded, waited on them, washed their feet and gave them the eucharist, despite the fact that beforehand some wanted to call down fire from heaven on the Samaritans, that one was already betraying him and a few minutes later others would abandon him in their sleep, and later their leader would violently sever a soldier's ear. (In fact, on an earlier occasion Jesus had even compared Peter to Satan for not heeding God's ways!) Jesus instituted the Holy Eucharist in the midst of His disciples' messiness and chaos!

Jesus welcomed this motley crew of stumbling disciples to their first communion table despite the fact that soon all but one would disown Him by running away from the cross. It would appear that most of the twelve, by any human judgment, would not have seemed exceptionally worthy or ready to receive their first holy communion. However, Jesus must have judged otherwise.

What of those who walk out of the ashes of failed dreams and shattered marriages? Some of these have been close to the church; they go to church regularly, raise their children in the church, and face the myriad problems of hectic lifestyles. Many of them hunger for the eucharist; they feel the need of the bread of life to sustain them on their journey. They also want some assurance from their church that meeting this need is justified. They may need an emergency accommodation if the strains of modern life keep increasing. They may need precisely the strength and the healing that come from holy communion.

THE WOUNDED DIVORCED

They need strength to survive because divorce leaves wounds. Some of these wounded ones have simply returned to Holy Communion, a minority have sought annulments, and a few have sought counsel from pastors through confession or counseling, and have returned to the eucharist.

In recent years, the Holy Father, as a pastor concerned for his flock, wanted the annulment process to be the normal means for addressing the issue of remarried Catholics. However, sometimes, when divorced people inquire of local pastors about a possible annulment, they are told, "I don't do annulments." What is probably meant is that this particular pastor is not well versed in advising the person about the writing of the necessary narrative history of the failed marriage. In such a case, the inquirer should find another pastor who is able to give the necessary help.

COMING HOME TO A NOURISHING CHURCH

Too often, remarried divorced Catholics tend to feel divorced from their church community as well. They sometimes drop out. They need to be invited home. According to Hoge's study, 23 percent of

Catholics who "leave active participation" in the church come home again to Catholic participation. These returnees need to find a warm welcome in our Catholic mess halls. Joseph Champlin, an articulate pastor, calls for a pastoral response to potential returnees, many of whom are "cold or hungry, frightened or discouraged." He suggests they need to come home to a nourishing church.

BACK HOME AGAIN

A group of such returnees gathered to discuss coming back. This group was quite diverse—various ages and backgrounds. The following is a verbatim account of their conversation:

When the discussion began, the oldest, a man in his sixties, asked, "What about a situation like mine, where I can't get an annulment because I am unable to gather the necessary testimony? I have been in a second marriage for years. Is there any way I can receive the eucharist?" Another responded, "I know people in my parish who do." The older man responded, "But I want assurance from the church that it is okay." Finally, the moderator explained, "The best thing to do in this situation is to have a private visit with your pastor, where he can get the whole story and advise you."

With that, the group seemed to relax a little. One, an attractive thirty-five-year-old woman responded, "Well, here we are talking all this through and trying to come to understandings about becoming active again, but what about the folks out there, just hearing about remarried Catholics going to communion, or who think annulments are just Catholic divorce and think the church is getting soft, aren't they liable to become very confused?

"Even within myself, there is a part of me, as I come back, that wants black and white structures with everybody in their legal place, like when we were kids and someone bent the rules in our games. We so quickly said, 'That's not fair!'

"Thinking that way is secure. In a way, I think we want to be adults, and yet in another way, we want yes-no rules, with no exceptions." She paused and sighed, and then added, "But I guess coming back, or staying in, or leaving the church ultimately has to be a big personal adult decision. And I am not really in a position to make final judgments on other people's decisions."

Someone on the other side of the circle added, "Yes, do you remember the first night we all gathered here? Our first question was, 'Well, we know the old rules, what are the new ones?'"

The moderator chimed in, "Yes, I guess there will always be rules. They make for order in our chaotic world. Maybe the rules are the fence around the sheepfold. They are there to protect marriage and families."

A woman responded, "But Jesus is the shepherd at the gate. It's my understanding that in danger of death, the church only asks for an act of contrition, and anybody from Mussolini to my Uncle Fred can be reconciled and receive the sacraments." (Laughter.) "Hey we are not Mussolini!—and not in danger of death either, I hope."

After the laughter subsided, the speaker continued, "Yeah, I kind of see it like the church has a rescue squad for emergencies. I think there are lots of emergency Catholics who need to be picked up and brought home—and the emergency is not just danger of death—it's just trying to get through the messiness of life. I've got to believe there must be a way to bring many home, if they want to come. We have made it. There are lots of others who we need to bring with us!"

THE SPIRIT BECKONS HOMEWARD

Paulist Father Alvin Illig, an expert on Catholic evangelization, has written that the Spirit would bring many of the millions of bruised and yearning unchurched back home if they were offered tact, sensitivity, patient listening and understanding accompanied by genuine love.

Other research by Gallup and Castelli about the unchurched or nonpracticing Catholics would seem to indicate that many of them are not so far out, or far away from being normal Catholics as they THEMSELVES might define themselves. Sometimes, some of the very attitudes that they possess and that they judge are causes for alienation from the church are the same attitudes that practicing Catholics also share! Unfortunately too many divorced Catholics define themselves as out, or think falsely that the church categorizes them as untouchable outsiders. This is a false assumption and self-fulfilling prophecy.

THE PASTORAL CARE OF JESUS

Jesus offered pastoral care and deep concern for the woman at the well who had suffered through multiple divorces. He asked her to serve him at the well, and he promised her living water. He gathered her into his circle rather than pushing her out. His disciples were amazed by this, but by his action he gave them and his church an example of pastoral care.

The fact still remains that at the present time a majority of aggrieved and divorced Catholics are not seeking a peaceful, canonically accepted return to the eucharist that could result through an annulment. The font of living water may be present there, but they are not lifting the ladle to drink.

IT'S WORTH THE EFFORT

Comments like these from persons who have gone through the annulment process indicate it is well worth the effort:

"I dreaded writing the narrative history of the courtship and marriage, but as I wrote it, I began to experience a healing of old, lingering, bad memories."

"The whole procedure put a closure on a painful chapter in my life and I've been able to move on."

"In our situation, the annulment process did not label either me or my ex-wife as 'bad.' Rather, it just validated the fact that we were just too immature when we married to really grasp the depth of the sacrament. I'm guessing there are an awful lot of other people like us, not villains of any sort, but rather people just not psychologically mature enough when they got married to contract a sacrament—a valid civil marriage, yes—a sacrament, no."

"My ex was not a bad guy, but I recognize now that when we married, he was sick—chemically dependent. There was so much denial about that. It was only when I got into Alanon and started the annulment process that I started to come out of the denial. Our marriage was not bad, but it was sick from the start. Sick enough for me to obtain an annulment."

OUT THERE

Sadly, there are many other Catholics out there with similar experiences. Some, like Billy at the swimming pool gate, feel left out and locked out. Some are receiving pastoral care and welcoming arms from fundamentalist churches. Out beyond the gate where Manuel fled through the night, where the Emmaus disciples walked on the road, where neighbors and friends make their messy life journeys—sometimes separated, sometimes remarried, sometimes alienated and spiritually hungry—there is a need for an inn to take them in. The road is messy and muddy. There is a need for a Catholic mess hall with a light shining in the window and a note on its menu—"Come to me all you who labor and are burdened. Come home again!"

PRAYER FOR DIVORCED RELATIVES AND FRIENDS

Jesus, you called the burdened ones to refreshment. Hear my prayer. Over and over, you were present to the hurting ones, the alienated tax collectors, the ostracized woman at the well, the wandering sheep, the lost lambs.

The loved ones I pray for are neither scoundrels, nor outcasts; they are beloved members of my family and my circle of friends. I know both the pain and the goodness that is in them. If I know so much, how much more can you see into the chambers of their hearts?

Jesus, show the way to those who hunger for the eucharist. Help them to

*find the way to your table. The disciples on the road to Emmaus were
running away. You caught up with them, walked with them, and broke
bread with them. I bring...*

_____ *[names]* _____ *to you in prayer.*

*They wish not to run away, but to run to your embrace. Good Shepherd, show them the way to the inn. Bring them home again so that
they might know you in the breaking of the bread.*

WILLIAM JOHN FITZGERALD

PRAYER OF SOMEONE IN NEED OF AN ANNULMENT

*O Lord, the pen weighs heavy in my hand. It bears the weight of years of
memories, some good, some pleasant, some filled with anguish and pain.*

*As you said to your Father in heaven, "Let this cup pass," so my temptation is to say, "Let this pen pass; let those memories remain hidden away
in the recesses of my soul." I know that writing a narrative of this failed
marriage will blur ink with tears. I dread the anguish.*

*You also said, "Take up your cross and follow me." For me, this pen is
now my cross. May it lead me beyond the tomb of failed hopes and
dreams towards resurrection and better days.*

WILLIAM JOHN FITZGERALD

SCRIPTURE REFLECTIONS

Gen 2:15–24	MARRIAGE AS AN ORIGINAL BLESSING
Mt 19:3–12	JESUS AND DIVORCE
1 Cor 1:27–30	CHRIST'S CONCERN FOR US IN OUR WEAKNESS
Mt 12: 18–21	BRUISED REED

6

Coming Home from the Cold
to Mother Church

The people who come to our churches seeking some of the sacraments or some other pastoral service are often caught in the storms of life...

A warm welcome reassures callers that they have in fact rediscovered their true spiritual storm home.

JOSEPH CHAMPLIN [18]

I remember an encounter I had as a newly ordained priest. I went strictly by the seminary book and a person went away weeping. Needing a storm home they encountered a glacier. Thirty-seven years later, I now realize that no matter how far out we are on the ice, or out in the cold, our hearts are made to come home again to warmth.

As Catholics, many of us need to come home from the cold to Mother Church. We need healing, for we are part of a wounding and wounded church. Some Catholics feel shamed, others confused. Generational tensions and post-Vatican II differences have shattered the pre-Vatican II illusion of being a lock-step, always sharply focused *Going My Way* Catholic Church. (*Going My Way* was a very popular pre-Vatican II movie in which Bing Crosby played a parish priest.)

We suffer from our own Catholic apartheid. There are some Catholic groups—Native Americans, Hispanics, African-Americans with rich and deep spiritualities which are not widely known. Yet, they have maintained their Catholic heritage in North America far longer than most other Catholic descendants of immigrants. We are spiritually impoverished by not sharing their faith stories.

Too often now, progressives and conservatives stand apart in opposing camps. They refuse to share common ground. More and more some women feel left out. Church experiences sometimes create situations where alienation withers hope. We are in need of a spirituality to get us through our messiness, and of a means to find our way home again. Some may even need a baptismal bill of rights, a ticket that would allow them their rightful seat on a lurching Catholic train that is someday bound for glory, but not yet arrived.

RECOVERING CATHOLICS

We are all recovering Catholics. Some of us are messed up on our way home to a messy church. The paradox is that our church, which is meant to be a blessed home of reconciliation, is sometimes, through some of its members, an agent of harmful alienation. Heavy-handed uses of authority, moral shaming, generational tensions, even clergy abuse can leave some of us anguished and feeling there may not be a place for us.

Paul Elie, writing in *Commonweal Magazine* about "marginal Catholics," points out that we sometimes judge the church's action by its own standards and it falls short, or we see our own actions not measuring up to what we would consider to be the actions of "real" Catholics. This may result in anguish, marginalization or alienation. Most of us are not knowledgeable about the messiness of church history. When we do become aware of both the glory of its saints as well as the woundedness of many of its popes, bishops, and laity as they limped through history, the paradox of remaining Catholic but still falling short of some of the church's ideals is more understandable.

THE CHURCH VISIBLE

Today, we live in a fish-bowl church. For the first time in 2,000 years, via cable television, we can view images of its good works and its warts, its glories, and its scandals. As these contradictory images flood our television screens, we discover that the life of our church is not a neatly framed still portrait, but sometimes a jumble of seeming contradictions.

Mother Church limps. Peter Hebblethewaite, who reported the post-Vatican II Church, remarked shortly before he died that mothers do not have to be perfect in order to be loved. Whether mother church or Mother Superior, or our own moms, rather than expecting perfection we have a right to expect from them just enough faith, hope, and charity to sustain us as we stumble along on our faith journey.

ALIENATION AND RECONCILIATION

Our church has a ministry to comfort us as a mother, but also to challenge us as brothers and sisters. We can receive great comfort through the sacraments of anointing, reconciliation, holy eucharist and through its rich and varied prayer forms, as well as through new small faith sharing communities of spirit companions.

But we are also challenged by the church's counter-cultural heroes and heroines who critique the prevailing culture, or whose witness goes against the grain of some secular values. Such witnesses can stir up in us an unease which might be called positive alienation. This kind of disquiet can call us to growth. We need the discomfort provided by people like our recent popes who critiqued both the sham of communism in the East, as well as the unbridled consumerism of the West. We need prophets as diverse as Dorothy Day, an apostle of nonviolence; Oscar Romero, living out an option for the poor; our women missionaries martyred in Central America;

and Mother Teresa who has given witness to simplicity and compassion. They make us aware that we are often messed up by the prevailing culture.

WOUNDING

Unfortunately, beyond a challenging kind of discomfort, alienation and wounding can be inflicted through shaming by authority figures, by misunderstandings, or by treatment received from fellow Catholics that makes us feel not at home in our own faith community. Yet, this is the very place we should always feel at home.

Alienation then, becomes a problem for all Catholics, for we are all the church, the people of God, and if the church alienates, then we all do. I should start with myself and you with yourself when considering church agents of alienation.

GOING MY WAY

On my way to the priesthood, the movies *Going My Way* and *The Bells of St. Mary's* provided idyllic images of priests doing good things and having all the necessary answers. (Maybe it's progress that the more recent Father Dowling television mysteries have Father and Sister sifting through messy situations and searching for clues to mysteries.)

I recall the 1950's and realize now that sometimes my own pastoral attitude toward women using birth control was much stricter than was my attitude toward excessive drinking, gambling, or smoking on the part of priests. In the sixties, my recognition of my own sinfulness and failings began to deepen my compassion. I shall never forget causing a beloved friend to cry because of my own selfishness. When my own drinking led me to the edge of alcoholism, and when on one occasion it led to hurtful results, I became keenly aware that the sins of a clergy person could have far more disastrous results than those caused by a poor woman at the end of her financial or psychological resources who resorted to birth control.

"Woe also to you lawyers! For you load people with burdens hard to bear, and you yourselves do not lift a finger to ease them." (Lk 11:46)

I began to realize that despite my white collar, I was a messy priest, ministering in a messy church. In the midst of messiness, I discovered compassion—a pearl of great price. Like other pearls it was coated with a messy covering and had to be pried loose from a hard shell.

SHAMING

When some of my classmates became active in the civil-rights movement, they were shamed by many of their fellow clergy. Shame or embarrassment was a way of bringing them down to our size. They were locked out from understanding, much like Billy was locked out and shunned at the swimming pool gate. It is so easy to cause shame. Sometimes it is unintentional. I shall never forget two encounters with young women whom I had taught in grade school and whom I ran into in the same month many years later. Chris approached me with a beautiful smile and said, "I'll never forget how you listened to me when I was thirteen and needed a male father figure. If you ever think about your value as a priest, just remember what a good and powerful effect you had on me." I still felt the glow of that encounter when shortly thereafter, I met a classmate of Chris's. It was a brief meeting; tears welled up in this person's eyes and she said, "I will never forget that unkind word you spoke to me that day in class." With that she walked away. I don't know what that word was. All I know is that for her, I was an agent of alienation, whereas for Chris, I had been a carrier of affirmation.

PRAYER REFLECTION—SHEEPGATE

Sheepgate? Or shark's tooth?
  the clerical collar
  inviting to safety
  or to battlement's edge?

Depends on who "Father" is,
(maybe who my own father was,)
  contradicting sign?
  reconciling emblem?

Long ago on ordination day,
  face down, on the floor,
  priests' finest hour,
  earth bound and humbled.

Since then, ascending higher,
  arches, altars, pulpits,
  tempted to really believe,
  Father always knows best.

But in their inner sanctuary,
  there is no rail
  to seal them off
  from wounds and wounding.

I pray that I might find
  a "pasture shepherd"
  in the midst of messiness
  on my way home.

WILLIAM JOHN FITZGERALD

Any of us can get hurt by the church. Any of us can cause hurts on behalf of the church. We are both a wounded and wounding church. New Catholics sometimes say, "What I have found in the church is great comfort. I love belonging to the Catholic Church. Why is it that so many Catholics whom I work with do nothing but bad mouth their own church?"

REFLECTION PAUSE

Who do you know nursing hurts from the church? Perhaps they were intentional, perhaps not. Bring that person to prayer; ask the Lord to find a healing way to bring the person home again.

HEALING

Sometimes, both clergy and laity need to come home again to experience healing and reconciliation. The sacrament of reconciliation, when celebrated in community, can offer laypeople a unique opportunity to see priests confessing their sins to each other before they act as confessors for the laity. That sight models and images a wounded church in which ALL are in need of reconciliation, reunion, and healing.

Perhaps we need other rituals to bring us home. A pastor in Tucson welcomes returning Catholics into a group called Alienated Catholics Anonymous. A retreat master tells of inserting a session on healing church wounds. It contains a ritual in which participants write down their own church inflicted wounds, and vested in alb and stole, the priest prostrates on the floor, as at ordination, and asks forgiveness. Many aches pour out, like the pain of being sexually, verbally, or physically abused, or feeling scorned because of sexual orientation, divorce, or a second marriage. Others are pained by significant persons leaving the church or by trusts betrayed. There are others less dramatic but still painful—women feeling second best in the church, spouses in mixed marriages yearning for intercommunion, persons shamed by sermons, sadness caused by slow progress in ecumenism. They write down a lot and often there is not enough time for them to write down all they wish. Bear in mind, these are people who have taken time out to be spiritually renewed at a retreat house! What of those who have not even begun to come home?

VATICAN COUNCIL I, II, III?

As we stumble along on our church journey, some lean towards Vatican III; others pull back toward Vatican I. There is a warp and tension in our church. Like a brooding spring storm that brings growth to parched land, the tension may be at the very edge of new growth. There is no growth without some rain storms, mud, and turmoil. To be a Catholic today, or in any era of history is to journey with and through messiness.

MORAL MINE FIELDS

Sometimes, we search for the moral compass point as we discern our way through a complex culture underladen with moral mine fields. The *1994 Catechism of the Catholic Church*, the most recent compendium of the Church's teachings, seems to hint at the complexity involved in our efforts to discern, and to choose what is in accord with a good conscience when we find ourselves in the midst of messiness:

Man is sometimes confronted by situations that make moral judgments less assured and decision difficult. But he must always seriously seek what is right and good and discern the will of God expressed in divine law. [19]

WHEN WE WERE LOST

And what of those who know in their hearts that they have not discerned? What of those who know they have made harmful and immoral judgments and actions over a long period of time? What of those who seem to have abandoned the church of their youth, those for whom the church seems far off? They need to hear the beautiful words from the canon of the mass of reconciliation that assures us that when we become lost God loves us more than ever!

They need to remember that there is a sacrament of reconciliation that exists not for the self-righteous, but for sinners. The words to be heard there are not words of recrimination. Whenever I hear the confession of someone who has been away from the sacrament for many years, my response is always, "Welcome home again."

It is never too late to come home, and we are never too far from home that we can't be found. The poet Francis Thompson compared Jesus to a hound dog relentlessly pursuing each of us. It is never too late for us to be seized by God's relentless love.

REFLECTION PAUSE

Bring to mind loved ones frantically running; bring to mind those who seem far away. Imagine the Lord patiently pursuing them, catching up to them, taking their hand and leading them back home. Commend them to His relentless love.

THE SEARCH FOR SPIRITUALITY

Beyond the year 2000, the majority of U.S. citizens and large numbers of Catholics will live in the suburbs. As a suburban pastor, I observed quite a few Catholics shopping for a parish as they might browse at the mall. They are attracted to congregations that welcome them. Many of them yearn for good preaching that connects spirituality to their daily life experience, and they keep looking until they find it.

They have been accused by some of cafeteria Catholicism—of shopping for easy answers. But as I observe their hectic lives, it is my opinion that many of them are seeking a different kind of treasure than the consumer society can deliver. There is a growing thirst for community and a spirituality that provides meaning in the midst of messiness and chaos, for the suburbs no longer wall out chaos. As gangs and violence creep into the suburbs, there is a dawning awakening that neither the swank malls nor suburban walls can isolate them from chaotic random violence.

The late spiritual writer Henri Nouwen, in an interview with Catherine Walsh in *St. Anthony's Messenger*, describes our American Church as deeply impacted by the problems of the western world: alienation, segregation, separation, loneliness.

PRAYER REFLECTION—ON THE WAY HOME FROM THE MALL

Let malls deliver what they can,
sights, sounds, movement, rush,
flocking, grazing, browsing.
Our journeys are more than
mad dashes from malls to garage sales.

Our hearts are made for treasures
buried in fields and mountains,
sunk in mysterious seas,
cached away in the depths of hearts,
needing to be opened.

Lord, deliver me from plastic control—
credit cards, and checkbook frenzy.
Help ME to be a top consumer item—
for those who hunger and thirst
for my care, my simple presence.

WILLIAM JOHN FITZGERALD

SUBURBAN SPIRITUALITY

The suburbs are filled with Baby Boomers, a majority of whom dropped out of the church while growing up. Among the Catholic boomers, so far, a minority are coming back, yet according to recent research, eighty-one percent of them, churched or not, still call themselves Catholic!

According to research by Andrea Williams and James Davidson and reported in 1996 in *Sociology of Religion*, many members of the post-Vatican II generation do not describe the church *institution* as an essential component of their faith. Being a good person seems more important than being a good churchgoer.

Still, the Spirit is stirring in the suburbs—even within what Williams and Davidson call a shift from an institutional world view to an emphasis on personal spirituality. In an article entitled, *With Babes In Arms, and Doubts In Mind—A Generation Looks to Religion*, Kenneth Woodward of *Newsweek Magazine* describes this movement as,

...a broad powerful trend, that esteems prayer over pot, self-discipline over self indulgence, family love over free love... [20]

A 1995 *America Magazine* editorial lists spirituality as the number one pattern of need that draws some suburbanites back to church.

KERRY

Kerry told me such a story. After twelve years of Catholic education, she drifted away. "It was an age thing, but also—it was an either/or way of thinking that if I couldn't understand about birth control—then I probably could not be a 'good Catholic.'

"After I literally journeyed all the way from the deserts of Arizona to the forests of Alaska, with a failed marriage to an alcoholic along the way, I discovered Alanon—a great healing circle. But it was not enough. Then, way up in cold Alaska, I discovered a parish that was warm and welcoming. I joined a prayer group where it was okay to be me, okay to be excited about the God I found around lakes and loons and even cactus.

"Three years ago, I fell down a flight of stairs—and I was given a sick spell, a time to slow down and get quiet. I read a lot and made a Jesuit retreat. These new varieties of Catholic experience, plus meeting welcoming and caring Catholics provided turning times for me. I began to feel like I was home again. It was a wonderful feeling—coming home.

"I read the other day someone criticizing smorgasbord Catholics. How come? Our Catholic table is a smorgasbord, and I love it. I've experienced the charismatic renewal, *Genesis II*, Ignatian spirituality, contemplative prayer, and it's ALL wonderful. I just get hungrier.

"And then there is the eucharist. We don't have a resident priest in our Alaska parish so a sister is our parish administrator. We can't have daily mass. When the priest visits, and we do have the eucharist, the smorgasbord is complete. It's all there. Why go anywhere else? I've come home. I am accepted as a Catholic where I am on my spiritual journey. It is so good to be home!"

Kerry is among those who got separated by growing up and thinking, "I can't belong." Now, she has found her rightful place.

WOMEN'S HOPES

After a recent first communion, one of the communicants approached the priest with a big smile, and announced very seriously, "Father, someday, I am going to be a priest just like you!" This seven-year-old's name was Jennifer. If she had asked, "Can I?" The answer would have been "No." Like Kerry, will she find her place in the years ahead?

Across the generations, Catholic women are reflecting more and more on finding their place, being at home in our male-run church. Suzanne, a recent twenty-two-year-old graduate of Kansas University, upon hearing Jennifer's hope to be a priest mused: "I feel bad for her. Somebody is going to tell her no. That does not disillusion me, however. My own spirituality does not depend on male categories; however, so many of my classmates have written off the church. I want to find a middle way between the radical feminists and some Catholic fundamentalists who seem to be anti-female. Maybe my classmates will come back—maybe not. They have a definite sense of alienation in a male-defined church. If there were women priests, we'd find more space, I think. I'm not bitter, but some are."

Dawn, a generation beyond, a few months before her death after fifty years in the church, seems to echo Suzanne: "I now know that my spirituality does not stand or fall upon male definitions of who I am. My spirituality is part of me; it comes from raising children, being a wife and homemaker, my career, my ministry, peace and justice activities, and in my struggle with cancer. My daily prayer, the sacraments, and faith sharing communities give me the support to live out my faith. Because I love the church so much, I am willing to remain a part of it and continue my efforts to help it change."

For what may be a growing segment of women, the position of women in the church is messy. Kerry, Suzanne, and Dawn are several examples of those making a journey through the messiness, and finding a way home. Their spiritualities in messiness seem to combine a strong sense of Catholic identity and faith lives that are rooted in their own human experience. They trust their own feminine faith lens. They avoid taking an either/or dualistic stance regarding their church membership.

This was affirmed by a 1992 *TIME/CNN* poll in which a majority of Catholic women polled favored women's ordination even though it was a subject closed to discussion in the church. Yet 64 percent of the women polled were content with the church's overall treatment of women. Other data in this poll and in research done by Andrew Greeley point toward a majority of Catholics liking to be Catholics.

However, it must be of some pastoral concern that some 36 percent were not satisfied with the church's treatment of women. That is a sizable minority. Will Jennifer's generation increase those numbers?

BILL OF RIGHTS FOR THE MESSY

When Jennifer does grow up, the church will probably still be messy in one way or another. It will always need a sense of spirituality to deal with messiness. As the *Desiderata* tells us, the universe is probably unfolding as it should, and we have a right to be here. So too we have a baptismal right to be a part of the messiness of a church that is unfolding, not unraveling.

Perhaps the folks who have not yet found their way home, the ones who are wounded, alienated, apart, inactive, or on sabbatical need a Bill of Rights for the Messy. Too many of them have a negative Catholic self-image as Kerry had. A bill of rights might assure them that even though they might be messed up, they could join the crowd in a messy church. In a world where Thomas Merton reminds us that "everything about us belongs to everyone else," a baptismal bill of rights might remind us that the church belongs to us, and we to the church. We can come home. I was reminded of this by two recent encounters. A middle-aged woman came to me and described how at age twenty-seven something happened in her life that made her think she could no longer "be counted as a Catholic." She had wandered to other churches seeking solace. Now in mid-life she was beginning to think maybe she could be counted after all. When I told her she had never ceased being a Catholic, but "Welcome home anyway," tears welled in her eyes. The very same day, a Vietnam vet revealed to me how after the chaos of that war he once thought he was lost to religion, but was now, years later, fully owning his Catholic heritage.

THE SPIRIT AND MESSINESS

Our journey home to a sense of spirituality through our messy stories can be energized when we realize that at Pentecost, and in every age since, the Spirit comes in the midst of messiness to empower us to struggle our way toward our true home. And when we truly are at home, wouldn't it be more likely that we would be more personally responsible for our faith? Rights give birth to ownership, and genuine ownership empowers responsible faith. This kind of growth can occur when we no longer think of the church as "them," but rather "us." And, when we are empowered to do what Jesus would have us do with our lives, we can be further strengthened for action when we are in fellowship and community with other Catholics.

The late Joseph Cardinal Bernardin expressed it this way:

The Catholic Church is not a club in which members remain in good standing by coming to weekly meetings and paying their dues. It is a community of faith, hope, and love. [21]

At a period of Church history in the early part of the twentieth century when some Catholics were defining other Catholics as less than Catholic or not Spirit empowered, Pope Benedict XV wrote,

There is no need to add epithets to the profession of Catholicism. It is enough for each to say, "Christian is my name and Catholic is my surname. [family name]." [22]

A BAPTISMAL BILL OF EMPOWERMENT FOR MESSY CATHOLICS

✦ I have been gifted, called, and received into the Body of Christ and the Catholic Church through my baptism.

✦ "Christian is my name and Catholic is my family name." My identity cannot be scraped off.

✦ My cry is not "Who am I?—God knows?"; rather, "God knows who I am."

✦ This is true of all my loved ones, whether married or divorced, whether mass goers, or stay-at-homes, whether close to church, or alienated. Our identity cannot be snatched away.

✦ To be Catholic means belonging to Catholics.

✦ I am baptized into this multifaceted church, a stew that is multi-racial, multi-national, multi-spiritual, a hobo's stew of every flavor, yet loyal to one Lord, one faith, one baptism.

✦ I belong to a faith community with an unbroken, 2,000-year-old chain of prayer.

✦ I am baptized into a church that in many places is growing at its grass roots toward a genuine both/and identity: male and female, progressive and conservative, local and international, left brained and right brained, contemplative and active, black, brown, red, and white.

✦ I belong to a gathering of saints and sinners all challenged to make heroic journeys of various kinds.

✦ I belong to a church with a fertile imagination whose lay artists dreamed the Pieta and Chartres cathedral; therefore a church that can imagine a new beauty for a new millennium.

✦ I belong to a church that is most Catholic when it cries: "All aboard!"—a 2,000 year long train that is sometimes moving, lurching, stopping, backing up, going through dark tunnels and ages, switching, huffing and puffing, but finally moving forward—a train bound for glory, but not yet arrived.

✦ This old train runs to Medjugorje and to Catholic Worker houses, to Lourdes and to base communities, to charismatic conferences and to Trappist abbeys, to the great outdoors and to prisons, to home and to school, to work and to church, to my hometown, and to Rome. This is not a dualistic rail line of either ins or outs, but rather a train for us. There is a car and a care for everyone. Our little engine is Spirit driven and angel guarded, and it can take us on a heroic journey and bring us home again.

PRAYER REFLECTION—JESUS CALLING US HOME

Our Memories
There is an old homecoming church hymn that reminds us when our life journey begins to seem hopeless, or when we fear we cannot make it alone, we shall hear the "voices of angels, tenderly calling us home." Yes, we are the church of the guardian angels—angels of God, our guardians dear, to whom God's loves commits us here. We need to ask the holy angels to bring home to church those on sabbatical, those angry at church, those with father-wounds from paternal fathers and church fathers, those who have thought there was no place for them, those who have drifted, those who are angry or bitter for any reason. Let them hear the voices of angels stirring up memories and gently calling them home:

> *home to flickering vigil lights,*
> *images of kindly saints,*
> > *Jude who never gives up,*

Anthony who keeps searching,
    and Theresa who comes bearing roses,
memories of Mary and May Crownings,
the smell of incense and fresh Easter candles,
to little girls in white communion dresses,
and little boys with folded hands,
to the fiery red of Pentecost, the soothing green of ordinary time,
the purple of Advent hope,
to our heritage—Mary's month of May,
    to the poor souls of November,
        St. Valentine's and St. Patrick's days,
            and all the times that are holy,
and back to the Bible upon whose pages are the fingerprints of
the saints of all the ages:
    Cecilia who sang its psalms,
        Jerome who translated it,
            John Chrysostom who preached it,
                Benedict whose monks preserved it,
                    Teresa of Avila who danced to it,
to sprinkled ashes, green palms, and veiled crosses,
to the crossed candles of St. Blase blessing our throats.
To burdened hearts being reconciled.
To the white robe of baptism and the white palls of
parents' funerals,
to the triple sign of the cross blessing our thoughts, our words,
and our hearts,
to the silent hush at the elevation of the host
when Christ rises up in the midst of our messiness,
to the priest's hand raised in blessing, not condemnation,
to images of Our Lady of Guadalupe, the Black Madonna,
and the Shroud of Turin.
To the American women martyrs of El Salvador—roses in the
wintertime,
to the messy crib and the empty tomb,
to forgiveness in the midst of alienation,

to Jesus in the "mess hall" where we know Him in the breaking of
the bread, and His real presence in the tabernacle.
Let us hear the voices of angels tenderly calling us home.
Let them lead us out of the cold to a warm church again.
And someday, may the holy angels lead us into paradise!
And the martyrs come to welcome us!

JESUS CALLING US HOME

Jesus tenderly calls us home—from our frantic strivings, from our restless wanderings, from our fractured hopes, from our dashed dreams and disappointments, from our sinful separations—to a church that is meant to be a shelter until we reach our final home in His Father's house and its many dwelling places:

"Come home again, Peter, from your bitter betrayal and deserted
heart."
"Come home again, beloved John, from your days of thunder and your
thirst for power."
"Come home again, Magdalene, from empty arms and hollow
promises."
"Come home again, Dismas, from grasping and groping to letting go
and letting be."
"Come home again, Samaritan woman, from false fulfillment and
empty promises."

Our Homecoming

Lord let me come home; let my loved ones come home; let those who are
farthest from home come home:

> *not to a stockade, but to a sheepfold,*
> *not to a court house, but to a house of prayer.*
Lord bring us home to church—not a building, but to a compassionate,
faith-filled and loving community.
I especially remember those who are far away. May they sense a need to
come home:

(Pause and bring into your prayer those persons you know most in need of homecoming.)

PERSONAL REFLECTION—OUR MEMORIES, JESUS CALLING US HOME, HOMECOMING

> *Which of the three prayer segments above, "Our Memories," "Jesus Calling Us Home," or "Our Homecoming" relate most to your experience or that of your relatives and friends?*

> *Do you know anyone who needs a Baptismal Bill of Rights? Who? Why?*

> *Do you agree with Kerry that there is a wonderful menu available for you in the Catholic Church? Where do you find it?*

SCRIPTURE REFLECTIONS

Lk 10:38–41	JESUS AT HOME WITH MARTHA AND MARY
Lk 5:27–32	JESUS AT HOME WITH TAX COLLECTORS AND SINNERS
Jn 11:1–11	JESUS GOING TO THE HOME OF LAZARUS
Jn 14:1–7	JESUS GOING TO PREPARE A HOME FOR US

7

Coming Home from the Moon to Mother Earth

[This world…] can be discovered only by a spiritual journey of one inch…very arduous and humbling and joyful by which we arrive at the ground at our feet and learn to be at home.

WENDELL BERRY [23]

On July 21, 1969, a human walked on the moon and we saw our mother earth, as we've never seen it—our home from afar! A heroic quest propelled us through the wild skies all the way to the moon. There the astronauts discovered more than they ever dreamed. Their vision quest glimpsed our planet as our home in space. When they returned, they knew as no humans had ever known that our earth is one household. For them and for us, our coming home story means getting down to earth.

On our way back from the moon (and the mall) we need to come home again to the earth beneath our feet, for we have become alienated from our earth home which is the very source of our life and growth. Another Berry, Thomas, a religious and ecological prophet of our day, in his book, *The Dream of the Earth*, calls the separation from the earth's natural cycles, a kind of "technological fundamentalism." This kind of fundamentalist mentality causes us to focus our narrow vision on our egotistical and tribal needs. It posits no connection between these narrow needs and the needs of the rest of our planetary household which includes the other species, the water, the air, the earth itself.

REFLECTION PAUSE:

> *Consider the children in your life. Take a few moments to bring their faces to your mind. What will we bequeath them? Many are beginning to feel that our adult generations are not only consuming more than we should but that we are poisoning their earth home. Is there any greater gift that we can bequeath than a healthy earth home? Is there any worse curse we can leave them than a toxic earth home? Our earth alienation is more than messy. The despoliation of the earth could mean the ultimate human chaos. We need a sense of spirituality that leads us home from chaos. We need to pray for our children's future.*

PRAYER FOR THE EARTH

His blessing covers the dry land
like a river,
and drenches it like a flood.

(Sir 39:22)

Come Holy Spirit who brooded
over the primeval turbulence,
and turned it to rivers and seas.
Lead us out of the chaos of our uncaring.
May our spiritual voyage bring us home—
to the sacred shore beneath our feet.

Come Holy Spirit,
Fill the hearts of your faithful.
Kindle in us the flame of your love.
Send out your Spirit,
And we shall be recreated,
And you shall RENEW THE FACE OF THE EARTH.

WILLIAM JOHN FITZGERALD

OUR BUSINESS WITH THE PLANET

Paul Hawken, in his book *The Ecology of Commerce*, indicates that at the present time, EVERY living system on earth is in decline and that we are assaulting the earth's biotic capacity to produce life. Consequently, he tells us that the PLANET'S business must be the business of business! It is not good business for a few to plunder the earth at the expense of the many. Large numbers of the earth's people in the southern hemisphere are chronically hungry or starving, while the rest of the population, largely in the North, control and consume 80 percent of the world's wealth. Wendell Berry identifies every American as being a contributor to the destruction of life on the planet because we accept as givens the technologies that cause havoc in the earth household. We don't bother to look either beyond or behind the products we consume. For those who claim the name of Catholic such a narrow vision contradicts our very identity, for Catholic means a world-wide sacramental people possessing a world-wide vision.

DESTRUCTIVE SYSTEMS

Diane Fassel and Anne Wilson Schaef, in their insightful book, *The Addictive Organization*, attribute some of this narrow vision to a white, patriarchal, male system which is destructive to people and the universe. This is a searing indictment of some of the basic attitudes of modern science and industry which have sprung for the most part from the ingenuity of white patriarchal think tanks. Is such a verdict tenable? After all, who would want to give up flush toilets or McDonald's? What current visionaries like Fassel, Schaef, Hawken, and the Berrys may be trying to tell us is that instead of only looking UP at McDonald arches, church steeples, corporate towers, and mushroom clouds, we also need to look DOWN at the earth beneath our feet. Unless our mother the earth is holy and stable, we are all Humpty Dumptys perched on crumbling walls.

Father Knows Best, the title of an old television series, may well have also been the motto of many patriarchal captains of industry and progress. Five hundred years after Columbus brought this attitude to America, we may be on the verge of a new discovery: "Father does NOT always know what is best!" Our mother, the earth, may know what is best for our healing, our well-being, and our future. It may well be that at this very moment, in the depths of what remains of the rainforests, she is giving birth to an herb that will some day cure cancer, if only that herb can escape our onslaught.

In the dawn of the new millennium, coming home to a sense of spirituality through our messy stories may mean that we recognize how we have fouled our nest. The only way home to common sense and a biblical sense of stewardship is through practicing a new eco-spirituality.

Fortunately, there is a growing awareness that our very health is tied up with the health of rainforests and other eco-systems. There is also a growing awareness that our SPIRITUAL life as well as our physical life is intertwined with the other species of planet earth. This deeper insight is sometimes called eco-spirituality.

In talking to children, I sense that many of them will be among the leaders in this rising consciousness. There is a stirring among our children. They see images of blackened, oil-soaked birds. They blink and say it should not be. Our little children are frisky pups and they KNOW about clubbed and bloody seal pups, and seedlings in the rainforest, torched and trampled, and they murmur, "It is not fair!" On a national level, a large segment of grade school children who were surveyed in 1994 in the *Weekly Reader Election 96 Program* of *Parade Magazine* cited "cleaning and protecting the environment" as their number one concern.

Animated films such as *Fern-Gully* are helping a younger generation establish a loving and respectful relationship with the rainforests and the earth and all its creatures. I noticed the children in our parish school becoming more knowledgeable about ecology, and the need to connect ecology and spirituality. Their school and religious education curriculum sometimes took them out of doors to experience the fertile earth and the changing seasons. The earth and all its wondrous creatures can TEACH and children can still learn:

> *But ask the animals, and they*
> *will teach you;*
> *the birds of the air, and they*
> *will tell you;*
> *ask the plants of the earth, and*
> *they will teach you;*
> *and the fish of the sea will*
> *declare to you.*
> *Who among all these does not*
> *know*
> *that the hand of the LORD has*
> *done this?*
>
> (Job 12:7–9)

Each fall we celebrated the Feast of St. Francis with an outdoor prayer service. To the Litany of the Saints we added the names of two of the most famous Native American Catholics, Kateri Tekakwitha and Black Elk who exemplify Native Americans' kinship with mother earth. Praying to the north, south, east, and west, the children assume a reverent attitude to the earth from which they came. After that morning prayer service, the teachers reported that the children were heard chanting refrains from the litany throughout the day.

Each spring, the sixth graders spent three days at the woods learning from mother nature and praying in her midst. Each day became a holy-day, echoing the threefold response of the preface, "Holy, Holy, Holy, heaven and EARTH are full of your glory!"

Hopefully these kinds of activities can help our children to come home to a deep sense of spirituality through the messy and chaotic environmental story. Our very religion needs to challenge them to move beyond the chaos of human hubris that fouls the nest of future generations. We need to teach them that eco-spirituality means making care for the earth a faith matter, a hope matter, and a justice issue. "It's not fair!" is a judgment most kids warm to, and they learn to apply it to what we are doing to mother earth.

ECO-SPIRITUALITY AND PRAYER

Eco-spirituality brings prayer into children's environmental concerns. We teach them not only about the seven sacraments, but also that in some sense, all of creation is sacramental, that is, God revealing. This kind of world view is potentially more powerful than environmentalism since it is powered by reverence and prayer. Prayer can move mountains—and might save them as well.

REFLECTION PAUSE

Reflect for a moment about your children or grandchildren. What kind of water do you want for them to drink? What kind of air to breathe? Do you want to leave them denuded forests, poisoned rivers, eroded fields? Of course not. The Lord's command to Moses should ring out in the ears of all the older generations:

I have set before you life and death, blessings and curses. Choose life so that you and your descendants may live.

(Dt 30:19)

To be pro-life in the widest sense is to be pro earth. Babies will be no more healthy than the milk they drink and the air they breathe. The earth itself is the primal womb for all living creatures! What can you do in your home, your neighborhood about recycling? about conservation? (I once knew an old Austrian immigrant who said the greatest status symbol in her village was the largest pile of manure in someone's yard! In our time a new consciousness ought to identify the best status symbol as the smallest amount of trash left at the curb for collection.)

Whether you have a garden, or only a potted plant, try spending some quiet moments with it, meditating on the wonder of the seed coming forth from the fertile earth.

RAVAGERS AND DESPOILERS
A new eco-spiritual consciousness is beginning not a moment too soon. For too long, ravagers and despoilers have interpreted both fatherhood and biblical dominion to mean domination and exploitation rather than caring stewardship for the earth and all its creatures.

THE **GODFATHER** IMAGES
The *Godfather* movies provide vivid images of a destructive, white, patriarchal, male system in its most corrupted and virulent form. We need to become aware that what the godfather did to his neighbors and city, we as a human family do to our planet and to all our neighbors who share our earth household. The *Godfather* movies showcased a worst-case-scenario in which a dominant, male-headship family, corrupted by greed and hubris, exerted iron-fisted control and exploitation.

On the planetary scene, the "godfathers" do what they please with the planet. "Father knows what is best!" and our mother the earth languishes. The result is a worldwide mess and "progress" toward chaos. The way out of our mess will demand a new discipline of caring.

CHAOTIC DUALISTIC THINKING

The dualistic attitudes portrayed by the "godfathers" mess up people and the planet. They even launch an attack on sacraments and the presence of God in our world.

There is a chilling scene at the beginning of the original *Godfather* movie. As members of the family stand at the baptismal font, celebrating the welcoming of a new child into the community of saints, the camera fades to a scene showing other members of the mafia family machine gunning people to death. In the background, the priest intones, "Do you renounce the glamour of evil?" The rest of the mafia family responds, "We do."

This response is the ultimate in chaotic dualistic thinking. It separates what happens in church from what happens in the real world. The two scenes are a scrawl of sacrilege and desecration. The life that is celebrated at the font is wasted in the streets. There is a schizoid separation between the church sanctuary as a holy place and the streets outside as killing fields.

This dualistic dichotomy is a horrible contradiction of what sacraments are all about. Sacraments are meant to give life and knit together relationships. These movie scenes break relationships down to the lowest common denominator. My tribe counts. Anyone or anything beyond my tribal boundaries are potential prey for violent destruction, which is sometimes wrapped in the guise of ethnic cleansing.

The Kiss of Death

We need to come home, not to the *Godfather*'s tribalism, but rather to our earth household. Coming home ought to mean returning to a welcoming embrace of God's blessed creation, not to a kiss of death. In our time, it seems as though the dominant, white, patriarchal families of corporations, nations, and consumer societies have visited upon our mother the earth the kiss of death. Mafia-like, we waste the planet. As Catholic Christians, we ought to approach the desecration of the earth from a sacramental perspective, for the despoilation of the earth means that we ultimately desecrate sacraments. This is so because Jesus revered and blessed the earth and its fruits. He took water, wine, bread, and oil seriously. Sacraments are meant to reveal the power and the beauty of God in our lives, not mankind's despoliation. To pollute the earth is to despoil water, oil, and bread—the essential elements of sacraments.

Holy Oils

Glistening, pure oil plays a vital role in every baptismal ceremony. Prior to the pouring of water, the priest prays a prayer of exorcism, setting the child free from original sin. He then traces the sign of the cross with the oil of catechumens upon the infant's chest. After the pouring of the water, the fragrant oil of chrism is traced upon the child's forehead, just as Christ was anointed priest, prophet, and king. What is going on here? What is this exorcism all about? What does the oil mean? Does it mean life, or death? It *ought* to mean that life is more powerful than death and that the beauty of Christ emerges out of the messiness of the human condition.

Ugly Oils

The desecrating scenes in the *Godfather* movie give only a hint of the far wider corruption of the oils and water needed for the sacramental administration of baptism. Not so long ago, as priests in churches throughout North America traced the pure, holy oils on the bodies of newborns, the hull of the *Exxon Valdez* burst open and spread choking, sticky, unrefined, ugly oil across the pristine beaches of Alaska. The brow of mother earth received the kiss of death.

Perhaps one of the meanings of the baptismal exorcism might be that newborns are called away from the results of original sin that cursed the original blessings of Alaska's shores. I often mention this when I celebrate baptisms.

Healing Oils

In our daily usage, almost every beauty aid and healing agent for the skin contains some form of oil. No wonder that the blessed oil is traced upon us by the church to reveal Christ's healing powers. In the sacrament of anointing, the priest takes the oil of the infirm and prays that through this holy anointing, the Lord would help us with the grace of the Holy Spirit. The Holy Spirit of God is at work through the holy and pure oil! Surely it is *not* the work of the Holy Spirit when oil becomes an agent of pollution.

Our Oil Addiction

It is easy to point accusatory fingers at Exxon way up there in Alaska and away from ourselves where we live. If we do that, we ignore our own personal role in changing oil from a blessing into a messy curse. North Americans are addicted to oil. We make up .04 percent of the world's population yet consume 40 percent of its gasoline.

We pay the lowest price in the western world for gasoline but we have been willing to pay a heavy price in lives to feed our oil addiction. Our dependency on Middle East oil demanded our military intervention in the Gulf War.

We are so determined to maintain our gas guzzling ways that we hide our heads in the desert sands and embrace the Saudis, the God-fathers of the Middle East.

The Curse of Smog

Los Angeles once had one of the most comprehensive electric rail systems in North America, only to be replaced by cars with one passenger—bumper to bumper on smoggy freeways. Is this progress or folly?

We do this despite the knowledge that fossil fuels may have a serious impact on global warming. Our oil addiction has changed the blessing of oil into a potential curse.

OUR OWN "**EXXON VALDEZ** CURSE"

It is not just an Exxon tanker or crowded freeways that have caused havoc. Much closer to home, the disposal of used motor oil by do-it-yourself oil changers poses its own problems. It was estimated in 1990 by the American Automobile Association that each year, twenty times the amount of oil spilled by the *Exxon Valdez* in Alaska is dumped into America's environment by do-it-yourselfers who fail to dispose of the used oil properly.

The AAA figured that 210 million gallons of used oil were annually being dumped in backyards, storm sewers, and landfills which can reduce soil production and contaminate surface and ground water. So the messing up of the earth with ugly oil is as far away as Alaska, and as close as next door.

NUCLEAR SHADOWS

On a global scale, the earth lies hostage to nuclear destruction and contamination. In 1996, sixty admirals and generals from around the world urged the elimination of all nuclear weapons. Among them was General Lee Butler, former commander of the Strategic Air Command who commented,

"These devices extract a terrible price even if never used. Accepting nuclear weapons as the ultimate arbiter of conflict condemns the world to live under a dark cloud of perpetual anxiety." [24]

NUCLEAR WASTES

Ours is also a society burdened with deadly nuclear wastes as a legacy for future generations. The movie *China Syndrome* rang an alarm bell about commercial nuclear dangers and the Chernobyl disaster should have given us a wake-up call, but are we listening?

MATERIALISM

In our modern era of longevity, the life expectancy of males in Russia is 57 years. One of the causes of such a diminished lifespan is thought to be industrial pollution, the legacy of atheistic Communism's materialism—a Godless ideology that viewed creation as lacking any spiritual dimension.

HOLY WATER

The essential material of baptism is of course holy water. A powerful prayer is said over this water asking that the power of the Spirit would give to the water "the grace of Your Son." Holy water is ultimately meant to be graceful in our lives. Whether it is tumbling down the mountains, leaping up in fountains, refreshing us in showers, water is meant to give us life. Instead, we are turning its blessing into a curse. Our polluted Love Canals bring the kiss of death. We are desecrating holy water which is an essential source of life for all creatures. As this is written, the Environmental Protection Agency estimates that four of every ten bodies of fresh water in the United States of America are too contaminated by sewage, disease-causing bacteria, fertilizer, toxic metals, oil, and grease to allow fishing or swimming.

Our Abortifacient Society

Our underground aquifers are gigantic wombs that hold within them the life of the planet. We live in an abortifacient society. Should we be surprised at the enormous numbers of human abortions in a society that poisons its own wells and aquifers and gives every indication that it is willing to abort life in the planet?

How does a spirituality in messiness apply to water? New creation can emerge from messiness and chaos provided that chaos is not unrelenting. Mud is a penultimate mess. So is the flood-tide of the Nile that replenishes fertility, and the flooded rice paddies of China that feed a nation. However, what we are doing goes beyond making a mess. We are punishing the waters with unrelenting chaos. Messiness and chaos can bring forth new creativity, but unrelenting chaos will bring extinction. Earth will not go away, but life as we know it might. If we kill the waters, we mess up the very chain of life. Life can only emerge from holy water.

We have a chaotic relationship with water. In the former Soviet republics, the Aral Sea has shrunk by two thirds. Nearly half of U.S. lakes and streams are endangered by pollution. In India, nearly 8,000 villages have no local water supply. Deforestation is an increasing factor in decreasing rainfall around the world.

THIS IS MY BODY – MY BLOOD

When Caesar Chavez ended his fast protesting the indiscriminate use of pesticides by grape growers, he received holy communion. How fitting! For to poison the water, the ground, the air where grapes and wheat spring up is to poison the very eucharistic body and blood of Jesus Christ! Catholics, who are a eucharistic people, ought to be in the forefront of a spirituality within messiness that is eco-spiritual. This kind of spirituality sees deeply into all matter and reverences the divine presence in the depths.

SPIRITUAL DISCIPLINE

If we, as Catholics, are to live up to our name, we must not only be catholic (worldwide) in our membership, we must also be world-caring. From all of our ancient disciplines, perhaps our tradition of fasting needs to be revived to help deliver us from chaos. We also need reflective prayer that connects us to earth concerns, and the healing grace of humor.

There is a tremendous grass-roots interest among many Catholics in the events that have occurred in Medjugorje in Croatia. Young people there have reported apparitions of the Virgin Mary. Pilgrims who have gone there have discovered a spiritual energy. Four words might sum up that experience shared by so many—Wow!, Ouch!, Aha! and Renew! At Medjugorje, surrounded by beautiful mountains and faith-filled people, pilgrims take the time to sense the beauty all around them. This rediscovery of natural blessings can be a "Wow!" experience. Grateful prayer can spring from "Wow!" experiences.

The message of the Virgin asks these consumers to pray and fast. Fasting of any kind is a letting go experience that creates an "Ouch!" reaction. Such praying and fasting may open the possibility for a raised consciousness for so many of us who are messed up at the mall. This might point us toward simpler lifestyles and more inner peace. Perhaps a wider view of fasting would help all of us and be a blessing for the earth. Fasting from inordinate shopping and excessive use of the gas pump might be just as valuable as fasting from food. It makes little sense to make a pilgrimage to Medjugorje to fast and pray, and then drive home from the airport in a gas guzzler!

Fasting might also mean turning off some of the estimated 350,000 commercials in our lifetime that manipulate us to consume more and more. Fewer trash bags at our curb might be just as pleasing to God as sackcloth and ashes! All of this might lead to an "Aha!" realization.

The "Aha!" comes from new insights and attitudes being created. Finally, the "Renew!" might signify a genuine transformation. A change of heart connects us to the eco-spirit, the Holy Spirit, the font of possibilities who dwells in the depth of our being.

The litmus test of any vision, pilgrimage, or new devotion might be if it nourishes a spirituality in the midst of messiness that is creative and that overflows into something new and good, not just for you but for our earth household. Thomas Merton describes this kind of spirituality as the highest form of life out of which our creativity becomes a source of action and creativity in the world around us.

REFLECTION PAUSE

Take a few quiet moments and consider the "Wow!"-evoking stimuli all around you, the beauty of friends, nature, the savor of life's little blessings the refreshing water of your shower, a smile, a warm cup of coffee, a wonderful memory. Make your own litany of "Wow!" experiences and praise God for all that is wonder-filled.

If we allow ourselves to be open to the natural "Wow!" experiences of fields and forests, sunshine and rain, and beautiful people all around us, we can rediscover awe and wonder. There are no two fingerprints alike in the universe! How awe inspiring! And each of us will leave our unique fingerprints and footprints on this planet as either a blessing or a curse for future generations.

If we enter "Ow!"—the cave of darkness, of imagination, and letting go, we can discover "Aha!"—new insights emerging from the messy but pregnant dark. New creativity can then burst forth in our lives and can become a new source of spiritual and transforming energy in our energy-depleting world. Creativity often brews in the dark.

EARTHY MARY

Catholics have a great reverence for the mother of Jesus. Her image is deep in our consciousness. It is interesting to note that almost wherever she is reported to appear, she does so close to the earth, near places of earth energy—springs, mountains, and woods. She is close to nature, not perched upon Eiffel, Trump, or Sears towers! Perhaps the medium here is part of her message. Male patriarchal cultures please pay attention to the voice of the feminine. It is close to the earth. Pay attention to mother earth. Fast and pray.

Through our busyness, our technology, our human self-absorption and our pop psychology, we have become alienated from our grounding, which is the earth. Part of our spiritual discipline demands that we pause; that we let go, in order to see the forest for the trees. We need to let go. We need to fast. We need to pray.

THE SAVING GRACE OF HUMOR

Another discipline, valuable for spirituality in messiness, is humor. The builders of the great medieval cathedrals added gargoyles to the outer buttresses. These were grotesque and comic figures. They did this for several reasons. They realized that only God was capable of perfection and so they acknowledged that they were imperfect builders. If the cathedrals are prayers in stone, then the gargoyles are prayers of humility—a word that comes from *humus* meaning earthy. The builders also had an intuitive insight that the demonic, the shadow side, was in some way mixed up with their human efforts. They acknowledged the chaotic element by way of the gargoyles.

Such gargoyles invite us to let go of human pretense, self-absorption, and hubris, and laugh at our messy human situation. Were they building today, they might put up gargoyles of present-day comics, or even of you or me. We would all be reminders of human messiness, some of which is laughable. If we can begin to laugh at our foibles, we can sense incongruity and begin to work through the messiness we have created. Only blind pride and human arrogance invite unrelenting chaos for ourselves and for our planet.

To slip on a banana peel invites laughter. To poison the earth, air, and water where a banana tree grows and to pass on poisoned fruit to our children is not laughable. We need to know the difference. Sometimes only laughter can alert us to our arrogance and hubris. The capacity to incinerate the world with atomic weapons is almost beyond imagination, but did appear on the drawing boards. The old movie *Doctor Strangelove, Or How I Learned To Stop Worrying and Love the Bomb* used macabre humor to get our attention. It is both foolhardy and laughable that we dare play Humpty Dumpty with the existence of life on the planet and consider it normal human activity.

COMING HOME WITH MARY TO OUR EARTH HOUSEHOLD
The themes of alienation, reconciliation, and healing have been threaded throughout this book. Whether it is Billy locked out at the swimming pool gate, or you and your loved ones locked out anywhere—we all need to come home again to ourselves, our families, our church, and to our earth household. We need to come home through our messy stories to holy ground.

You will sail the salt seas over,
And then return for sure,
To see again the ones you love,
And the Holy Ground once more
— TRADITIONAL IRISH BALLAD [25]

"HOLY GROUND"

The first lock-out at the Garden of Eden was the result of the ultimate alienation which is sin. But even after Eden, when our first parents were told to make a home on earth, the command of God was to "till the ground," not to kill it! In time, a new eve—nourished by the holy ground of Galilee—became the mother of everlasting life. Bone of her bone, and flesh of her flesh, Jesus, the Lord of the new creation came to be with us in our messiness and to deliver us from unrelenting chaos. Surely, we who love Mary, His earthly mother, should be the first to cherish our mother the earth, for we cannot love one without the other.

LITANY OF OUR LADY OF THE EARTH

Our Lady of Nazareth… (Pray for us.)
Our Lady of the gentle hills of Galilee…
Our Lady of Mount Carmel…

Our Lady of the Cana wedding…
Our Lady of the well-drawn water…
Our Lady of the sparkling wine…

Our Lady of Guadalupe…
Our Lady of the roses in the wintertime…
Our Lady of the humble peasant land…

Our Lady of Lourdes…
Our Lady of the lovely Pyrenees…
Our Lady of the healing spring…

Our Lady of Chimayo…
Our Lady of the healing earth…
Our Lady of the native peoples…

Our Lady of Medjugorje...
Our Lady of the holy mountain...
Our Lady of the peaceful valley...

Our Lady clothed with the sun,
the moon under your feet,
you were with us
in the primordial fire-ball,
every element of your body and ours,
and all the stars together!

Draw us into kinship
with soil, plants, and moving creatures.
Let our spirits rejoice
with "Ohs!" and "Ahs!" of wonder
at the earth—a nurturing cradle
for your everlasting Son!

WILLIAM JOHN FITZGERALD

PERSONAL REFLECTION—OUR LADY OF THE EARTH

Our Lady was closest to God's son and closest to the earth. Which verse of the Litany of Our Lady of the Earth appeals most to you? Why?

"Mafia-like, we waste the earth." Where is this happening closest to you? Is there anything you can do about it?

"Holy Oils, Holy Water, Holy Earth": What is your reaction to the statement, "We must approach the desecration of the earth in a sacramental way."

Which chapter in this book most addressed your life concerns?

How can a spirituality in messiness help you in your life?

Scripture Reflections

Gn 1:6–10	God saw that it was very good.
Ex 30:31	Holy Oils
Is 24:3–5	The pollution of the earth
Jn 9:1–7	Jesus uses mud to heal.
2 Cor 5:17 & 18	We are new creations.
Rom 8:18–22	Creation's messiness is creative.

Notes

INTRODUCTION

1. Genesis 1:1, 2, New Revised Standard Bible, Division of Christian Education, National Council of Churches of Christ, U.S.A. (London: HarperCollins, 1989 [as are all subsequent scripture quotations]).

2. Arnold Mindell, *The Year I* (Global Process Work, Penguin Group, Viking Penguin Inc., 40 West 23 St., New York, NY 10010, 1989), p. 113.

3. *Order of Christian Funerals,* International Committee on English in the Liturgy, ICEL translation, 1970, (The Liturgical Press, Collegeville, MN 56321, 1971), p. 64.

CHAPTER 1

4. David Steindl-Rast, *Gratefulness, The Heart of Prayer* (Paulist Press, 997 Macarthur Blvd., Mahwah, NJ 07430, 1984), p. 6.

CHAPTER 2

5. Sydney Carter, *Lord of the Dance*, Shaker song copyright 1963 Steiner & Bell, London, England admin. by Hope Publishing Co. contained in *Breaking Bread*, Today's Missal Annual Music Issue, published by Today's Missal, P.O. Box 18030 Portland, OR 97218, 1995, #514.

6. *Zorba the Greek*, Director, Michael Cacoyiannis, scripted from the Nikos Kazantzakis novel, Produced by Twentieth CenturyFox, 1964, distributed by Fox Video, 2121 Ave. of the Stars, 25th floor, Los Angeles, CA 90067.

7. Terry Anderson, *Resiliency of the Human Spirit Address* Scottsdale, AZ Franciscan Renewal Center, Feb. 9, 1995.

8. William Barry S.J., *Discernment in Prayer, Paying Attention to God* (Ave Maria Press, Notre Dame, IN 46556, 1990), p.82.

CHAPTER 3

9. *Parenthood*, Movie Producer: Brian Grazer; Director: Ron Howard. Imagine Films Entertainment Inc., 1925 Century Park East, 23rd Floor, Los Angeles CA 90067, 1989.

10. Ibid.
11. Mary Richards, *Centering in Pottery, Poetry, and the Person* (Wesleyan University Press, 110 Mount Vernon St., Middletown, CT 06459, 1989), p. 30.
12. William J. Fitzgerald, *Speaking About Death* (ACTA, 4848 Clark St., Chicago, IL 1990), p. 37.
13. John S. Donne, *The Way of All the Earth* (Macmillan Co. 866 Third Avenue, New York, NY 10022, 1972), p. 220.

CHAPTER 4
14. *"Recovering Together"* (Good Samaritan Hotline, Vol. III, #10, P.O. Box 8642, Scottsdale, AZ 85252, Jan. 1994), p. 6.
15. Jane Fonda, *Remembering Dad, TV Guide*, Division of News America Publishing Co. Radnor Corporate Center, Radnor, PA 19088, Jan. 11, 1992, p. 11.

CHAPTER 5
16. John Steinbeck, *The Acts of King Arthur and His Noble Knights,* from the manuscripts of Thomas Mallory and other sources. Edited by Chase Morton (Farrar Straus & Giroux, 19 Union Square West, New York, NY 10003, 1982), p. 288.
17. "Marriage and Divorce—Is it time to crack down on easy divorces? *CQ Researcher*, May 10, 1996, Vol. 6, #18, p. 413, Congressional Quarterly Inc., 1414 22nd St., N.W., Washington, DC 20037, p. 411.

CHAPTER 6
18. Joseph Champlin, *The Marginal Catholic—Challenge, Don't Crush* (Ave Maria Press, Notre Dame, IN 46556, 1989), p. 85.
19. *Catechism of the Catholic Church*, © 1994 Libreria Editice Vaticana, Citta del Vaticano 1994, p. 440, #1787.
20. Kenneth L. Woodward, "With Babies in Arms and Doubts in Mind, a Generation Looks to Religion," *Newsweek,* 251 West 57 St., New York, NY 10019, Vol. 116, #25, Dec. 17, 1990, p. 50.
21. Joseph Cardinal Bernardin, *Homily,* Aug. 21, 1982, Chicago Tribune Publishing, 435 N. Mich., Chicago, IL 60611; Nov. 7, 1996, Special Section 2, p. 3.
22. Pope Benedict XV, *"Ad Beatissimi Apostolorum,"* Nov. 1, 1914, published in *The Papal Encyclicals,* 1903–1939, Claudia Carlew, IHM (The Pierian Press, P.O. Box 1808, Ann Arbor, MI 48106, 1981), p. 149.

CHAPTER 7
23. Wendell Berry, "The Unforeseen Wilderness" from *The Earth Speaks* (Institute for Earth Education, Warrenville, IL 60555, 1983), p. 181.
24. General Lee Butler, "Outlook, Disarmament, Brass Vs. Nukes," *U.S. News and World Report,* 2400 N St. N.W., Washington, DC 20037, Dec. 1996, p 12.
25. Traditional: Irish Sea Chanty.